Geometric
Beadwork

By Jean Power

Geometric Beadwork is written and published by Jean Power
www.jeanpower.com / Copyright © 2012 Jean Power
ISBN 10 - 1542891892
ISBN13 - 9781542891899

First Edition - published November 2012
Second Edition - published January 2013
Third Edition - published November 2015
Fourth Edition - published February 2017

Printed by CreateSpace

There are many people I would like to thank who have helped this book to come to fruition:
- Everyone who supplied beadwork, proofed instructions or tested projects for me. You provided more help than I can ever thank you for
- Everyone whose wonderful photos help to make up all the eye-candy contained within its pages, especially Kyle Cassidy, Martin Norris, Jeroen Medema and Kate McKinnon
- Alison Smith for helping me design the book and making sense of my scribbles and instructions
- Lynn Davy for proofing and support
- All the beady friends I have made along the way. Your friendship and support means the World to me
- Special thanks go to everyone who put their faith in me and pre-ordered a copy of this book. Without you it would not have been possible

Please note that I have tried my best to ensure that these instructions are accurate but if you spot any errors, have any queries or would like to show me photos of anything you have done from the book (and I would love to see them!) please contact me through my website at www.jeanpower.com

Welcome

Let's be clear right from the start that I know nothing of maths, numbers or geometry....

...just the thought of these fill me with dread, yet when I pick up a needle and beads I find my hands settle into adding corners and angles to my work without me having to know my times-tables.

When you read this book, and the instructions within, be assured that knowledge of Pythagoras is not essential to create geometric beadwork. All I ask is that you have a desire to explore and create new and exciting work, which is how all of this started.

My first geometric project began by accident, when I had no idea what I was doing. I took that accident and spent years working on the principles I learnt from it in order to create all of the work you see in this book.

Pictured here is my first true geometric project and I hope you can see how it gave rise to everything you'll find within these pages.

My desire for this book is to pass on knowledge I have gathered while beading and fill you with inspiration to take that knowledge and create work that grows from your own hands and becomes truly yours.

This book is laid out in order of progression through shapes, ideas and difficulty, with each project building on the techniques in that section and ideas developed in previous projects.

I would recommend that before you begin any project, you make sure you're familiar with the techniques it refers to. This is not wasted time – it will save you lots of head-scratching when you bead the project, and just experimenting beading samples using the basic techniques can lead to all sorts of wonderful variations.

But don't feel you have to be regimented or bead one thing in order to bead another. Look through the book, see what catches your eye, dive in and before you know it you'll be creating geometric beadwork…

Jean

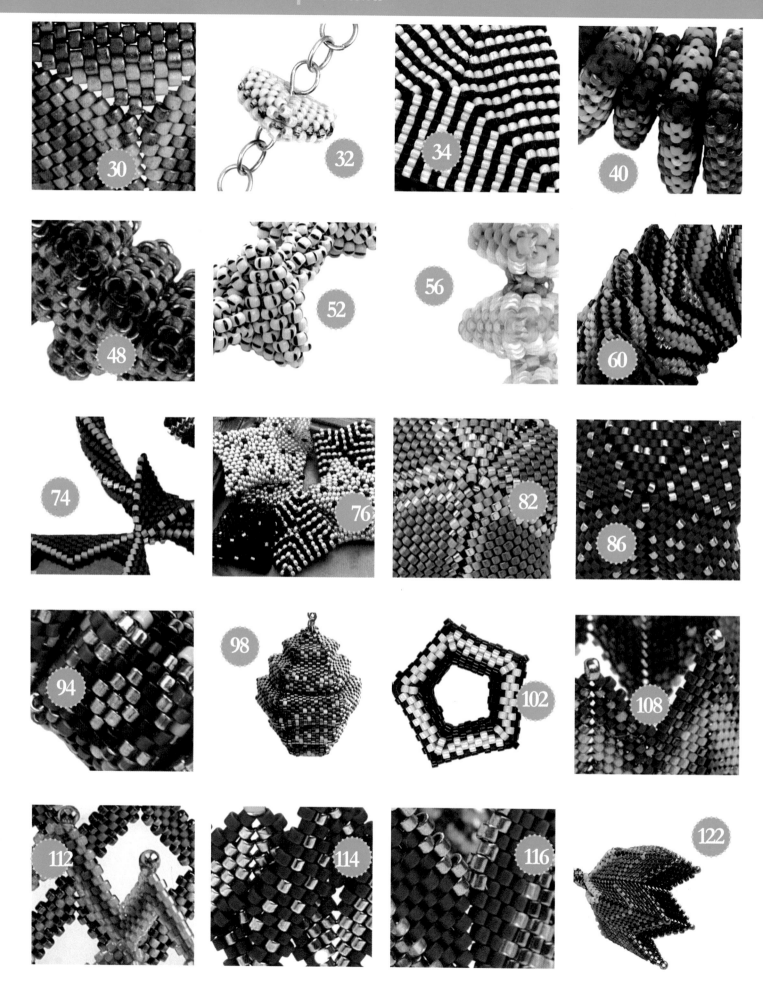

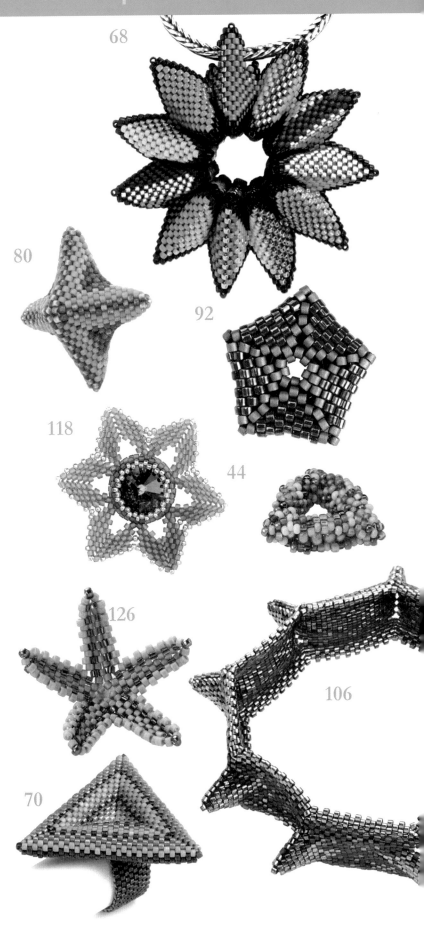

Basics

Triangles

Squares

Pentagons

Corners

Basics

Get started with all the
basics needed to complete
the projects within...

Terminology
All the techniques, terminology and tips you'll need to create your own geometric beadwork...

Back through
This means to thread through a bead in the opposite direction than you previously went through it

Corners vs. side spaces
When you bead a distinct geometric shape (such as a triangle or square) it will begin to develop two different types of spaces: corners and sides.

Corners are where all the action happens. It is these spaces where you will increase or decrease to alter the size of the shape.

Side spaces just have one bead added into them, and their quantity increases as you continue to increase your work.

However, as soon as you start increasing or decreasing in a side space it becomes a corner...

Step-Up
This is the practice of ensuring you finish a round by threading through, usually but not always, the first bead added in that round. Sometimes the specific bead you need to thread through will be different, but a Step-Up is always needed at the end of a round.

If you do this your work will begin to spiral and one side of whatever shape you're making will always be shorter than the others. This may not seem a problem at first but will soon become one when you carry on beading

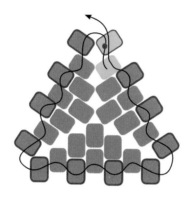

In this diagram, to perform the Step-Up, you would need to thread through the two blue beads

It can be easy to miss your Step-Up, and only thread through the first bead of the round, not spotting that you need to go through two, as has been done here

Point Round
When you have finished increasing, and need to add a round with a single bead in every space, this is the Point Round

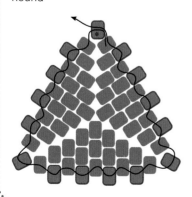

TOP TIPS
Beware the 'hiding' Step-Up. See 'Tips' for more details.

To help you see your Step-Up, it can help to count out all your corner beads before you begin a round i.e. 6 beads for a triangle.

Circle through
Circle through means to thread through a bead (or beads) in the same direction that you previously went through it

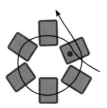

DB
Whenever DB is used in this book it refers to the manufacturer's code number for a Delica bead

In a nutshell!
This will tell you the basic steps needed to complete a project in this book

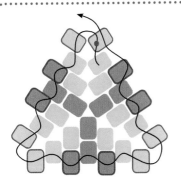

Herringbone Increase

This is a method of increasing in peyote stitch by adding two beads into one space, just as you would in Herringbone Stitch. In this diagram, all the blue beads were added using Herringbone Increases

Stitched on

Occasionally you'll need to stitch on a bead. This means to use ladder or square stitch to attach one bead to another. This newly added bead will be referred to as a 'stitched on' bead, such as the blue bead in this diagram

Row vs. round

Rows are for flat beadwork, where you weave from one side to the other. Rounds are for circular and tubular work, where the beginning and end are right next to each other

Beads per side

It can be tricky to count rows or rounds in 3-dimensonal work, so instead I count beads. This I do by counting the beads that sit along one edge of my work. In this diagram I would say this triangle was '5 beads per side'.

I use the same method when decreasing, so I would say I had decreased this triangle down to '2 beads per side'

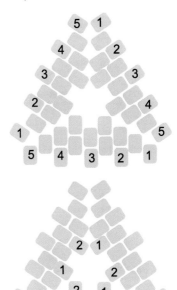

Out, in, up, down...

Adding single beads in spaces means you're neither increasing nor decreasing. Whereabouts you add these single beads, what you're beading and even how you think about your work will alter their effect.

You can think of this as adding length (on a rope), adding width (when making beaded beads or beading side panels on shapes) increasing depth (making circular bangles or Rick-Racks). You can even think of it as the piece growing upwards or downwards (depending on which way you're holding it!)

However you think of, it the result is the same...more of the same

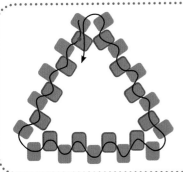

Peyote Decrease

A decrease in which you follow the same thread path as you do when using Peyote Stitch, but don't have a bead on your needle

Splitting a pair

When you add any beads between a pair of beads added in a previous round this will be referred to as 'splitting the pair'. In this diagram, each pair in the second-to-last round has been split with a single red bead added in the last round

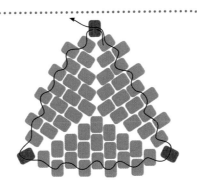

Spaces vs. gaps

Beware when following the instructions that, unlike regular peyote stitch, where you add beads in spaces formed by the previous rounds, in geometric beadwork you will sometimes need to add beads into gaps between beads, such as in this diagram

Tips
Relax...remember, this is meant to be enjoyable!

To knot or not
I don't tie a knot when I begin my work; instead I simply thread through the beads I need to join my work into a circle (but only once). I believe that tying a knot holds the work too tight and doesn't allow the beads to settle down and find their own space as you continue. The only time I make an exception to this is when I want my work to be too tight e.g. Distorted Squares

Tail Thread
Beadwork is tricky to hold when you start a new project and I find having a long tail thread, which I wrap around my fingers, helps with this immensely. It also means you can return to the start later if you need to. It will also help you to control your tension and stop beads falling off the end of your thread...

Impact
It's important to understand that as you bead all future work will have an impact on what has gone before. This is especially true when decreasing as it can take a few rounds of further work to pull those first few rounds tight and into place. So bear with it, extra beading adds extra thread, extra substance, extra security and extra shaping, all of which have a bearing on the end result

Losing your shape
You've worked hard at increasing a triangle, beaded a Point Round and are now merrily beading along with 1 bead in every space when suddenly you notice that instead of a triangular tube you have a round tube...

- This is because what makes a tube triangular (or square or pentagonal) is the shaping beadwork done at either end, i.e. the increasing and decreasing.
- Too many rounds of 'plain' beadwork, i.e. just single beads in every space, will mean your work soon turns into a tube.
  There are a couple of ways you remedy this:
- Increase and decrease often. Even if it's only a single round of decreasing and then increasing back to where you were, this will return your work to the shape you want
- 'Ladder a ridge.' Identify the beads that sit in the 'corner spaces' on every other round of your tube. Weaving through these, as though linking them together with Ladder Stitch, will help pull them into a ridge and emphasise the corners of your shape

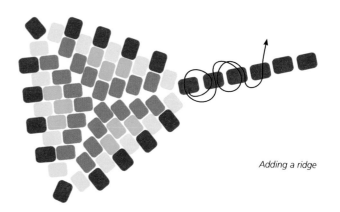

Adding a ridge

The rule of 2
Whenever tying anything into a circle, and I know I'll want to return to my start later, I thread through 2 beads to begin. Immediately the tail thread is ready to just pick up and carry on with later

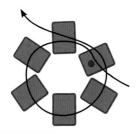

Steps-Ups hiding from you
Be aware that as you work, especially when you decrease, your Step-Up may be moving around with every round (this is to be expected). Even when it seems you don't have a Step-Up you will, it just may not be so obvious or it may come after you perform a decrease rather than the last bead of a round.

For example, in this diagram the blue bead is the last one added, but the Step-Up doesn't occur (into the yellow bead) until after a decrease is beaded at the corner

EXPERIMENT!

❝ This is how you'll learn new things and create your own projects. 'I wonder what will happen if I...' is the best question you can ask yourself as you work. Trying and seeing what does happen can lead to great things ❞

Think of it like cooking...

When you begin you don't know much about the different ingredients, utensils or techniques. You soon learn that every oven is different and that you need to keep an eye on what you're doing if you want a good result.

The more you cook, the more you learn and before you know it you can open the cupboard and just know what delicious dish you can make with the ingredients you have to hand.

Think of beading in just the same way and you'll soon be able to look at a tube of beads, contemplate a corner and know more or less before you even start what will result when you put beads to thread.

I'll let you in on a secret...

Whenever you reach a space, or want to add a bead, you need to make a simple decision: 'How many beads shall I add here?'

That's it - that's the secret to all of this work.

How many beads you add affects the results and what direction (literally and figuratively) your work goes in.

So, all you need to bear in mind is:

- **Do I want to carry on as I am?** (That is stay steady, stop growing, bead a tube, create some length or width) Then add 1 bead
- **Do I want to increase?** (Do I want to grow a wing, horn, corner, or just head off in another direction) Then add 2 beads
- **Do I want to decrease?** (Shrink, turn inwards, reduce, bead the other side of a horn, wing or corner) Then add no beads

> **TOP TIP ... LOOK AT YOUR WORK**
> *This really is my top tip! As you bead, look carefully at what you're creating. This is how you'll learn what effect the different things you do will have. All this knowledge will sit at the back of your mind and help you with your future work*

Stop bead

Adding a stop bead at the start of work can be really helpful, not only to stop beads falling off the end of your thread but to also help you control your tension. To add one simply circle through a bead a few times, without splitting the thread. When you've finished just remove the thread and the bead

Diagrams

The diagrams in this book follow a set pattern:

- The first new bead in a round is identified with a circle of colour
- All the new beads added in a step have a different colour outlining them
- 'Greyed out' or 'faded' beads are those which sit behind the beadwork the current steps are showing

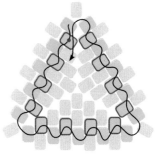

Materials and Tools

There are very few essentials you will need to use this book, but here are all those I can't live without

Beads

Where it all begins. Most of the projects in this book are beaded using cylinder beads, which are shaped like small sections of a tube (in contrast to seed beads, which resemble doughnuts with their curves). Cylinder bead is the generic name and some brand names are Delicas, Aikos and Treasures. This style of bead is perfect for geometric work as their flat sides sit neatly next to each other and their exact sizing and shape mean your work will be very regular.

Cylinder beads also have very large central holes which mean you can thread through them many times and also use knots to start and finish thread.

Once only available in one size (size 11) you can now get cylinder beads in sizes 15, 11, 10 and 8 all of which are great for using in your work. See page 14 for examples of altering bead sizes to alter your work.

Thread

Once you've chosen your beads your next most important material, the one that holds it all together, is your thread.

There is so much that could be, and has been, written about beading threads but I'm going to keep it short and sweet - use what you love. I prefer small reels of Nymo as I find it doesn't tangle on me, it's nice and strong and there's no coating to come off, But that's my personal preference and experience and I know many others who would disagree with me on all counts!

So, when it comes to threads my top tips are:

- Use what you love. If it works for you, stick with it
- Experiment – you may just find that some threads work better for some projects or beads than others. You won't know until you try
- Remember that thread is probably your cheapest component and should be treated as such. Never re-use it and cut it off as soon as it looks even slightly damaged and fluffy
- Always stretch your thread before you start beading. Not only does this help to stop your work from sagging later but it reduces it tangling as you work. As you remove it from the reel or cone pull it between your hands until it's straight

With their flat sides cylinder beads are pefect for creating neat, angular work

Rounded seed beads create more rounded work

Bangle Sizer

This is the perfect tool for making a piece that fits over your hand and sits nicely on your wrist. Imagine it as a metal belt and you can see how it works. I ignore the measurements on it instead choosing a size which squeezes onto my hand (your beadwork will be more flexible than the sizer, meaning the sizer can be set to the smallest size possible). The sizer is also great for measuring your progress as you go so you can see you are getting somewhere.

Thread

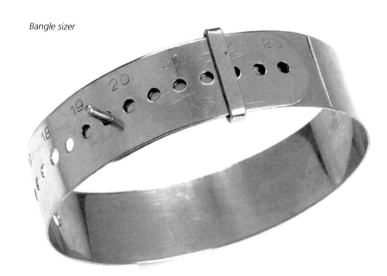

Bangle sizer

Bases for your beadwork

I'm not a big fan of clasps on my beadwork. I struggle to find any which suit it or that I love; and of course I don't want anything to distract from the beads themselves. But if you don't want to have to make all your jewellery continuous, or just want the ability to interchange pieces and play with looks, then metal bangle and neck wires are great. I use the ones where one end unscrews and the piece itself can be bent to adjust the opening and sizing. They're great when used for big pieces, such as the Bold & Beautiful necklace on page 52, but also for beaded beads and smaller work.

" These are the things I find essential but you may find your perfect toolkit varies from mine "

" The last important tool are needles and I always use the thickest I can as I find this a lot less tiring to bead with. Fortunately the large holes in cylinder beads make this easy to do "

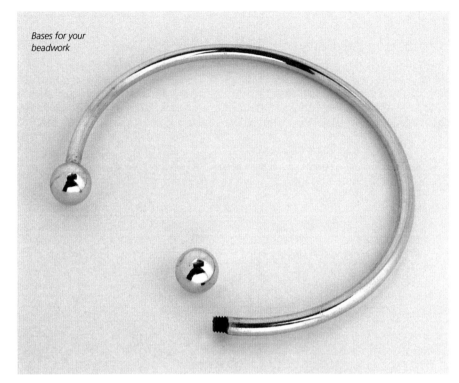

Bases for your beadwork

Bead Breaker

After being introduced to this I can't live without it! You use the push pin (which gets fatter towards the base) to break out a bead. It's much better than pliers as it explodes the beads outwards, making it less likely to cut your thread. The eraser is partly to make it safe when in your bead bag and partly so you can press into that rather than your hand or a table

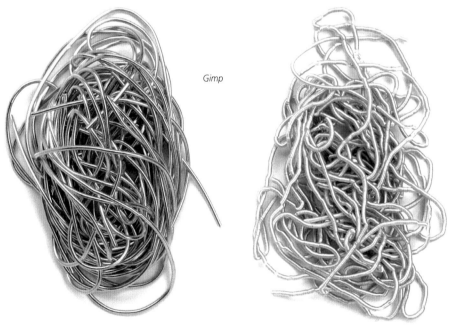

Gimp

Gimp

If you are going to use metal clasps on your work then you can use gimp to help protect your thread from rubbing and wearing. Gimp resembles a very fine spring, but with no stretch or spring to it, and is designed to cover your thread and keep it safe. Do make sure you experiment with it and treat it carefully as it can be fragile and tricky

Colour and Design

There are so many ways you can play around with the ideas in this book, but here is some advice on how to use colour and design in your work

Bead colour

You only have to look at the pictures in this book to see just how much the colours of your beads can really affect how a project looks.

My preferred way of choosing colours is to simply dive in and see what happens – this often works, but not always!

Bead finish

This is my real hot button beading-wise. I understand how much we all love those shiny metallic and silver-lined beads, but if you overload your work with them you're making a big mistake.

It's a simple fact that your eyes don't like shine. Think how a sudden glare hurts your eyes and makes you squint or turn away. If you make your whole piece with shiny beads, no-one will be able to see the beautiful detail of your work, and beading will actually be a lot trickier and more tiring for you.

So save yourself time and tiredness, and make your geometric masterpiece more effective, by adding in lots of matte beads or even just 'ordinary' opaque colours. The finished result can still look shiny and not dull, but the contrasting bead finishes will make the colours and details stand out far better.

Bead size

A great way to alter a design is to scale up or down the bead sizes you use. Most of the work in this book is done with cylinder beads, which are now available in sizes 15, 11, 10 and 8 – all of which can be used to create any of the work featured. But of course if you do want to alter the bead size you may need to alter the number of rounds or rows that you bead if you want the piece to be the same physical size.

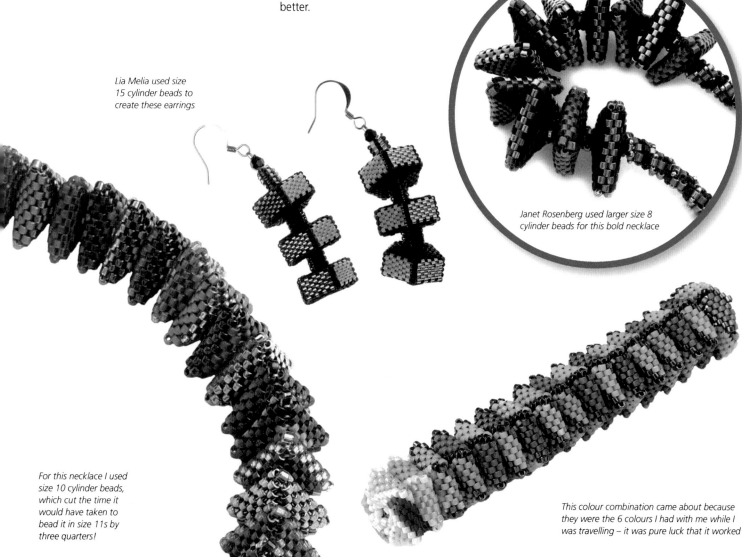

Lia Melia used size 15 cylinder beads to create these earrings

Janet Rosenberg used larger size 8 cylinder beads for this bold necklace

For this necklace I used size 10 cylinder beads, which cut the time it would have taken to bead it in size 11s by three quarters!

This colour combination came about because they were the 6 colours I had with me while I was travelling – it was pure luck that it worked

Rose Rushbrooke used the wonderful quilt she created as inspiration for this dramatic bangle

Finding Inspiration

If you're stuck for a colour choice, then look around you. Not only are there wonderful choices in nature, but your own possessions, pages from magazines and even household products can all be used to inspire your choices.

Right: Dana Steen Witker mixed dots and stripes in her dramatic stars

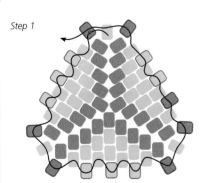

Step 1

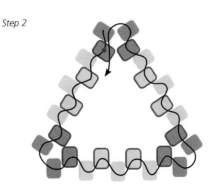

Step 2

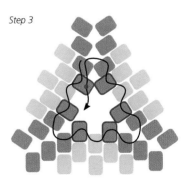

Step 3

Planning Ahead

Sometimes you'll need to be thinking a few steps ahead with your colours; this is especially true when making a piece using lots of increasing and decreasing, such as the Caldera Bangle on page 60. This is also important when adding patterns such as stripes of colour which follow the Herringbone Increases; see the Triangle Holes pendant on page 68 for an example of this. Although it's very easy to make sure you add your Herringbone Increases in one colour on the way up, it's not so easy to spot where to put the colour as you're decreasing. The trick you need to remember is: add the different colour bead as the first and last bead on a side, right before and after the corner decrease. See these three diagrams for examples of where the colour needs to change

Patterns, dots and stripes

I love making patterns in my work and most of them come about after me pondering 'I wonder what happens if I change colour here?' Try it yourself and see what happens.

Faces and Sides

Some of the projects you'll make are reversible (such as the Reversible Pendant on page 34) and some, such as Power Puff bangles, can have 3 sides. Take advantage of this and play around, as I have done in the as yet unfinished bangle on the next page.

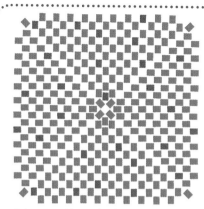

Dots not touching each other

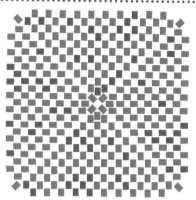

Colours placed randomly when I don't mind if they touch

Dots

To create these I simply add in beads of a different colour whenever I feel like it. If I only want dots then I make sure I don't touch that colour bead with another of the same colour at all, but if I don't mind, then I place them randomly

Dana Steen Witker used turquoise seed beads for the Point Round on her star for a wonderful look and texture

When beading stripes which you want to repeat on your decreases you need to think ahead

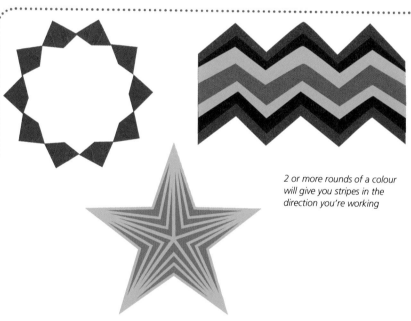

2 or more rounds of a colour will give you stripes in the direction you're working

Stripes If you change colour after two or more rounds, then you will have a stripe going in the direction you're beading (remember when making Distorted Squares this will look different depending on how you use them).

However, if you change colour every round then your stripe will go at right-angles to the way you're beading

Single rounds of colour will make your stripes go at right-angles to the direction you're working

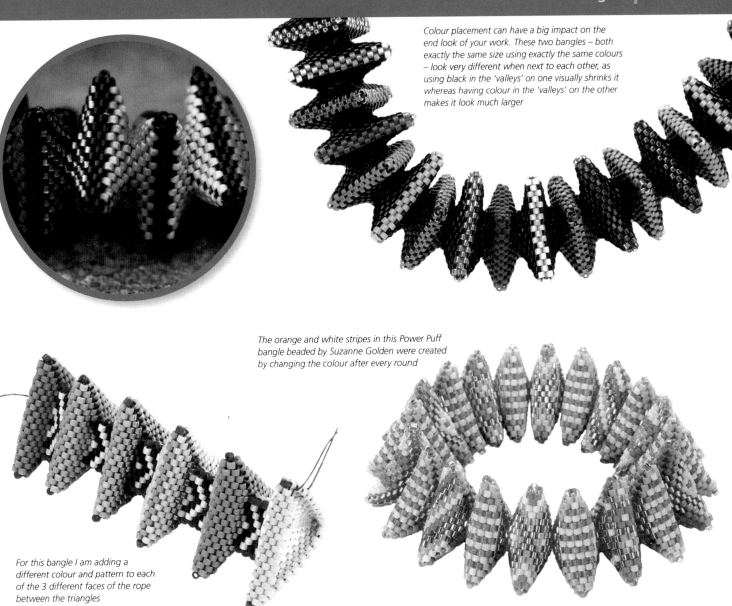

Colour placement can have a big impact on the end look of your work. These two bangles – both exactly the same size using exactly the same colours – look very different when next to each other, as using black in the 'valleys' on one visually shrinks it whereas having colour in the 'valleys' on the other makes it look much larger

The orange and white stripes in this Power Puff bangle beaded by Suzanne Golden were created by changing the colour after every round

For this bangle I am adding a different colour and pattern to each of the 3 different faces of the rope between the triangles

This version of a Caldera Bangle by Shona Bevan only uses 7 colours (plus black) but because where the colours sit moves around, it looks as though so many more were used

Play with ideas
There's no reason a bangle project in this book has to remain a bangle for you. The pendant on page 68 began as a bangle but I soon realised I could turn it into a pendant instead, so let your imagination run wild!

Play with placement
Just because a pattern specifies 3 colours doesn't mean you can't use 2, or 7 or even just 1. It all depends on what you're making and the end result you're after

Different beads
Using completely different beads than stated will give you a really different look – which may be just what you want. However, if you just want a subtle addition of different beads and a different texture, then a sprinkling is a great design feature

Peyote Stitch

Peyote stitch is based on the principle of creating spaces, and then filling those spaces with beads. This book doesn't contain the basics of learning peyote stitch – there are many others far better for that – instead it focuses on using certain aspects of peyote stitch to create geometric and 3-dimensional beadwork.

Flavours of peyote stitch

Peyote stitch comes in many forms: circular, flat, tubular… and these can all be either odd or even-count.

This book mainly uses tubular and circular forms of the stitch, and always even-count (that is using an even number of beads/spaces to begin, so that each round finishes with a Step-Up).

But it's not even

Don't worry if sometimes you seem to pick up an odd number of beads to begin something; you will probably be performing a Herringbone Increase at some point, which means you'll use a gap between beads to add new beads, making your work even-count.

First rows and rounds

In peyote stitch the beads you pick up at first will determine the width of your work and form the first and second rows or rounds of your piece.

Circular peyote stitch to create geometric beadwork

STEP 1
This is beading which goes around in a circle, usually with 1 bead added into one space.

STEP 2
At the end of every round you will Step-Up to exit the first bead added in that round and be ready to continue.

STEP 3
In order to keep your work flat and even, you sometimes need to increase your work by putting 2 beads into one space, such as the gold beads in this diagram.

STEP 4
Usually you would then split these double beads in the next round and make sure that any further increases didn't happen on top of the previous ones so that your work remained circular and even…

STEP 5
…however, in geometric beading we want to use these increases, and the way they distort the beadwork, by placing them right on top of one another and creating corners, horns…

> *The basics of peyote stitch and geometric beadwork. Every project in this book is based on this simple stitch and this basic idea*

 Step 1
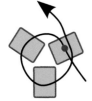

 Step 2

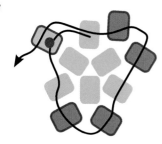 Step 3

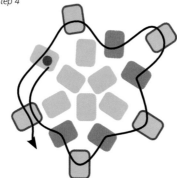 Step 4

 Step 5
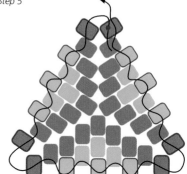

Herringbone Increases

A Herringbone Increase is made by adding 2 beads into any space, or gap, in order to increase the width of your work, add a corner, horn, petal or wing. It can be added anywhere you want it; continuing to add increases one on top of the other is what will shape your work.

"It is these increases which alter the shape of your work and make it geometric"

Increasing in a peyote strip

Bead peyote stitch as required, then when you reach the spot you want to increase add 2 beads instead of 1.

When you bead the next row, when you reach the previous increase, exit the first bead of the pair, pick up 2 beads and then thread down the second bead of the pair. Continue beading the rest of the row, adding any further increases as required.

 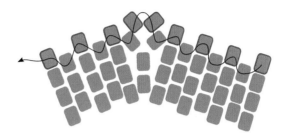

"Don't panic right away if your work doesn't seem to want to lay flat. It may be just what you need (see Distorted Squares on page 74) or it might take a few extra rounds to make it sit right"

What Next?

An increase is added by using 2 beads in a space instead of 1 and when you return to that space on the next row, or round, you exit the first bead of the previous pair. What you do next depends on whether you want to add another increase (in which case you add 2 more beads) or if you want to stop increasing (you add just 1 bead)

Increasing in circular peyote

If beading a piece of circular peyote then you can add Herringbone Increases into any of your spaces. If you continue increasing on top of increases you get corners and from this you can make geometric shapes.

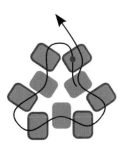 

"There are other methods you can use to increase so feel free to experiment"

Point Round

The Point Round in your work is used to end any increasing or to add a neater-looking edge to a piece, in which case it's optional.

It's simply beaded by adding just 1 bead into every space, including on top of all of a previous increase.

These two diagrams show a Point Round being used to end two different types of increasing or shapes.

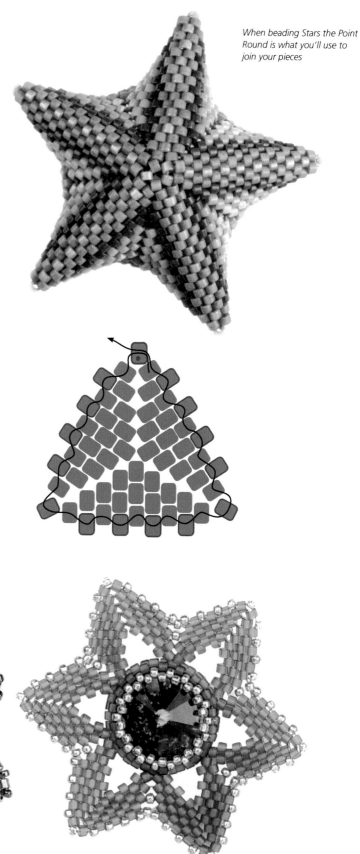

When beading Stars the Point Round is what you'll use to join your pieces

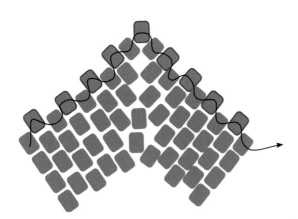

A Point Round in seed beads is used to finish the edges of these flowers

Decreasing

A decrease is what you'll bead when you want to reduce your work in any way; also when you want to add tailoring, or bead the 'reverse' side of a corner, wing or horn.

It is beaded by simply threading through your work as through you were beading a single peyote stitch, but with no bead on your thread,

These diagrams show you the decrease happening at the corner of a piece and also within a piece so you can see how it is exactly the same no matter where you use it.

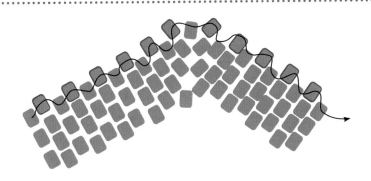
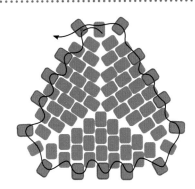

Starting to decrease

Just as with all types of decreasing, you first need to add in a row, or round, which has a bead either side of the space you want to decrease in the next row. So, bead a row, or round, with 1 bead in every space, which will become your first row, or round, of decreasing.

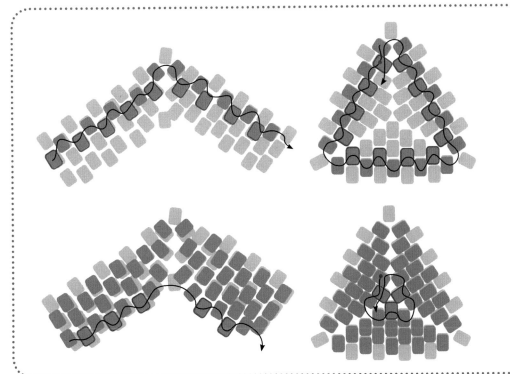

Continuing to decrease

On your next row, or round, thread through your work using regular peyote stitch but when you reach the spot where you want to decrease (exactly where you increased previously if you want them to match up) don't have a bead on your thread. Instead make sure you pull tight to bring the two beads you're threading between together.

Continue decreasing using this method, making sure when you get to a corner/where you want to decrease, you add nothing and thread across between the two beads that stick out either side of the decrease which stick out, until you have gone down as far as you require.

Trying to zip together the ends of this piece would be very hard

Zipping and Joining

Zipping your beadwork is how you'll join separate pieces together and also how you'll unite ends of the same piece

Preparing to zip

Before you can zip pieces together, they need to have the correct number of rounds. Generally you don't want each piece to be the same size (as in the 1st diagram) as then the 'teeth' beads will meet face on rather than slotting together.

Instead you want to add a Point Round to one piece (as in the 2nd diagram) which will let them unite as desired.

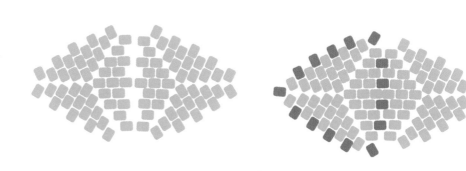

This end of beadwork, by Kate McKinnon, will be much easier to zip together now

How to zip

Simply weave between your two pieces of work, threading through the beads in the last round of each one (these will be the ones that stick out more).

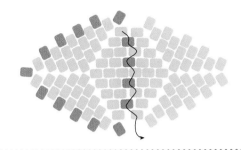

Continuing to zip

If you're going to carry on adding pieces then you will need to fill in the Point Round all the way around the second piece in preparation for the third being able to unite with it.

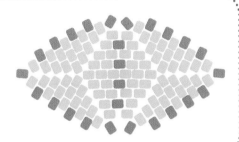

Zipping in a valley

A lot of the beadwork within this book is created as a tube and the ends are joined together. However, this can result in your trying to zip up your work in a 'valley' or other tight space.

It is much better to remove the rounds at the start of your beadwork and add subsequent rounds to the end of your work so you are zipping along an outside edge.

Zipping along an outside edge is much easier than zipping down in a valley

Zipping and joining is what makes a Star a Star. On this piece the Point Round was beaded another colour so you can see where the Distorted Squares are zipped together

Widen Your Horizons

When you make shapes with larger central holes the same principles of increasing and decreasing apply - you simply begin with more beads. These instructions will explain the basic principle but if you want to begin with a little more guidance then check out the projects on pages 40, 44 and 102 which all use the principle but with step-by-step instructions.

Linked work
If you want to make your shapes linked together then make sure you join your beads into as circle in Step 1 through your previous work

THE STEPS...
STEP 1
Your starting beads
As the inside of the central hole will be a tube (it may be a very small tube!) of circular peyote stitch you want to pick up an even number of beads to start, and then ensure your number can be divided by the number of sides you want your piece to have.
- So, a triangle needs to divide by 3, but be even, so any quantity of beads you begin with must be a multiple of 6 i.e. 6, 12, 18, 60, 180…

- For a square you want a number that is divisible by 4 so 4, 8, 16, 40, 80…
- For a pentagon you need an even number that is divisible by 5 so any multiple of 10 will do: 10, 20, 30, 40, 100, 150…

STEP 2
The central tube
Next you'll add at least 1 round of plain circular peyote to this central hole (this can be done now or later). You always need an odd number of rounds in the centre so your corners match up but that can be 3 rounds, 5 rounds, 17 rounds…

STEP 3
Calculating your corners
Once you are happy with the depth of the central section you'll begin to increase and place your corners. Working out where these sit involves a bit of maths - sorry!
To calculate it you need to:
- Halve the number of beads you picked up to begin (this gives you the number of beads per round)
- Divide this by the number of sides your piece will have (so for a triangle divide by 3, a square by 4 and a pentagon by 5; his gives you the number of beads per side.

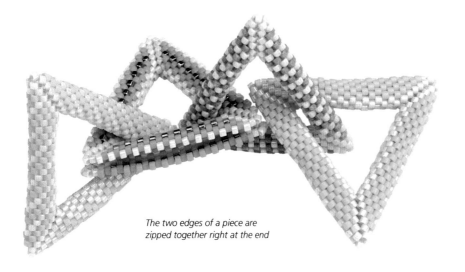

The two edges of a piece are zipped together right at the end

So, if you begin with 12 beads and you're making a triangle you'll end up with 1 corner and 1 side spaces (12/2 = 6 then 6/3 = 2). So you will add 1 corner with 2 beads and then a single bead in the next side space. Repeat this twice more to bead all around your round

So, if you begin with 24 beads and you're making a triangle you'll end up with 1 corner and 3 side spaces (24/2 = 12 then 12/3 = 4). So you will add 1 corner with 2 beads and then a single bead in the next 3 side spaces. Repeat this twice more to bead all around your round

So, if you begin with 560 beads and you're making a pentagon you'll end up with 1 corner and 55 side spaces (560/2 = 280 then 280/5 = 56)

Variations
If you want to add extra 'depth' to the outside of your pieces (see the pentagon beaded bead variations on page 94 for an example of a project with more depth to the outsides of the shapes) then simply bead an even number of plain circular peyote rounds, with 1 bead in every space, after you have beaded your Point Round in Step 4. It needs to be an even number of extra rounds that you add so that the edges of your work will zip together correctly in Step 4

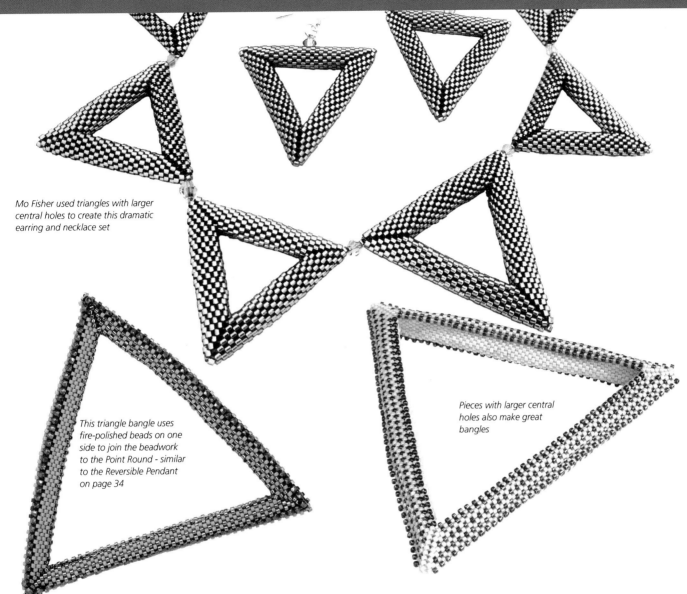

Mo Fisher used triangles with larger central holes to create this dramatic earring and necklace set

This triangle bangle uses fire-polished beads on one side to join the beadwork to the Point Round - similar to the Reversible Pendant on page 34

Pieces with larger central holes also make great bangles

❝Adding a larger central hole to your work gives you much more room for variation in your project❞

- One of these will be your corner and the rest will be your number of side spaces

STEP 4

Beading the first side

Once you know where your corners belong, begin to bead one face of your shape. This is when you'll add in the Herringbone Increases and you can add as many rounds as you want.

Once you're happy with the number of rounds you've beaded, you need to bead a Point Round - adding just 1 bead into each space.

STEP 5

Beading the second side

Next weave back to the first round; right back to those beads you picked up in Step 1. If you want to add any extra rounds to add more depth to the centre you can do this now. Remember you always want to add a total of an odd number of rounds so you will need to add new rounds in twos.

Bead the second face of your shape ensuring that you place your corners in the correct positions so each face matches.

Once you have beaded the same number of increasing rounds, zip your edges together by threading through the Point Round beads previously added in Step 4.

In a nutshell!

- Choose what shape you wish to make and pick up an even number of beads that divides by the number of sides in that shape
- Bead an odd number of rounds of circular peyote
- Increase your shape as much as desired then bead a Point Round
- Return to the start of your work and increase your shape on this side
- Zip the edges of your work together

Triangles

Begin your fantastic geometric journey with three-sided shapes, so simple to create but so full of potential...

Beading a Triangle
The simplest of all shapes to bead - a joy!

Increasing a triangle

THE STEPS...

STEP 1
Round 1 - Begin with 3 beads. Join them into a circle by circling through the first one again.

STEP 2
Round 2 - Bead this by adding a Herringbone Increase into each gap between the beads in Round 1. This forms the corners.

STEP 3
Round 3 - Add another Herringbone Increase on top of each one in Round 1 - this continues to increase the corners. In every other space add 1 bead; these are the side spaces.

STEP 4
Round 4 - Add another Herringbone Increase on top of each one in Round 3 and 1 bead into each of your other side spaces. Note that there are now 2 side spaces along each side.

STEP 5
Round 5 onwards - Continue this pattern (adding a Herringbone Increase on top of each one in the previous round and single beads into every side space) until you have increased as much as you want to. Note that the number of side spaces will increase with each round.
   Point Round - Bead a round with just 1 bead in every space

Step 1
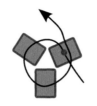

Step 2
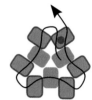

Step 3
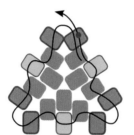

Step 4
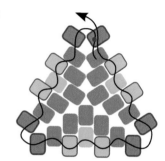

Step 5
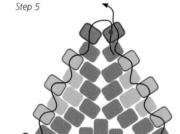

Step 5 - Point Round
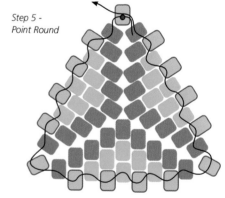

In these diagrams all the beads added in pairs are gold and those added singly are blue

Decreasing a triangle

THE STEPS...

STEP 1

Round 1 - As with all corner decreasing, you need to bead at least one round of 'regular' peyote stitch, with a bead either side of the corner space, in order to have a corner space to decrease in.

STEP 2

Round 2 - Bead another round of peyote stitch, but thread through the corner spaces without adding a bead. i.e. make a Peyote Decrease. The beads in your previous round will pull into the centre, but this can take a few rounds until it sits comfortably.

STEP 3

Round 3 onwards - Continue beading and decreasing by not adding a bead in the corners until you have decreased as much as required

Step 1

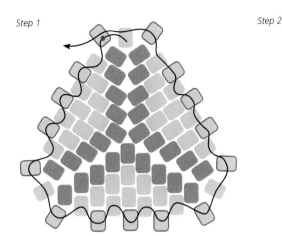

Step 2

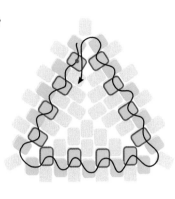

Step 3a

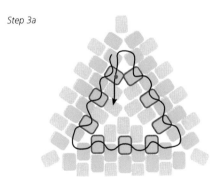

Step 3b

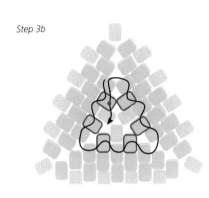

Step 3c

Flat Triangle Bangle
The basic flat triangle can be turned into jewellery with a few simple tricks

Joining flat triangles together makes an interesting, and easy, bracelet perfect for playing around with colours

Materials
To make one bangle measuring
6 ¾ inches/17cm when worn
- 5g size 11 cylinder beads
- A 5-loop slide clasp
- Gimp (optional)

Sizing
Sizing is going to be an issue with this bangle. As it needs an even number of triangles to make it work, you can't simply add or remove single triangles to adjust the length.
- If you want to make it longer then you can either add at least 1 extra round to each triangle, or use longer loops to attach the clasp
- To make it shorter then bead fewer rounds
- Using a different clasp, or beaded fastening, will mean you can play around with the sizing a bit more

Variations
If you want to alter the look of your bangle, then the colours and the number of rounds you use for each triangle is the first place to begin

Techniques
- Beading a Triangle, page 28
- Zipping and Joining, page 22

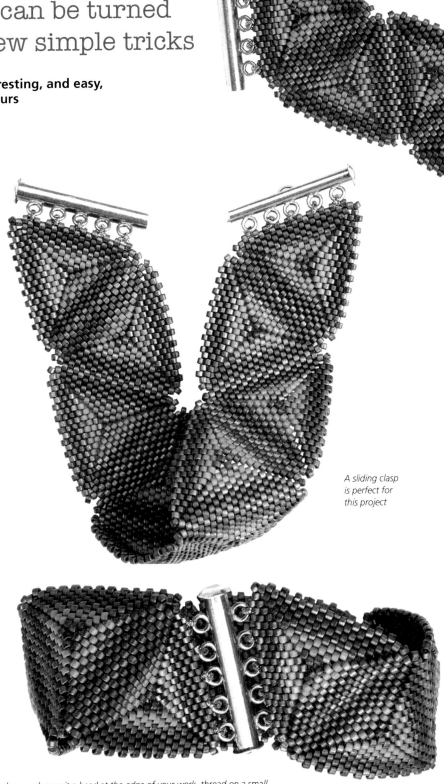

A sliding clasp is perfect for this project

To attach your clasp exit a bead at the edge of your work, thread on a small section of gimp, thread through a loop in your clasp and then back into the bead you were exiting from the other end

In a nutshell!
- Bead 10 triangles each up to 10 beads along a side
- Add a Point Round to the first triangle
- Zip the second triangle to the first then fill in the rest of the Point Round
- Repeat to join all 10 triangles
- Add a clasp, using gimp if desired

Tiny crystals add a touch of interest and sparkle in these quick to make beaded beads

Crystal Triangulations
The simplest of beaded beads jazzed up with a hint of sparkle

Materials
To make one beaded bead
- 1g size 11 cylinder beads
- 15 x 2mm crystal rounds

Variations
If crystals aren't your thing then you can simply use a different coloured cylinder bead, or a seed bead, to add texture

Techniques
- Beading a Triangle, page 28

I used
- Cream – DB203

Sizing
These beaded beads have only a very small threading hole, so if you want to use a thicker stringing material try the beaded beads with a larger hole on page 40.

> "These beaded beads have a small threading hole which makes wire a perfect stringing choice"

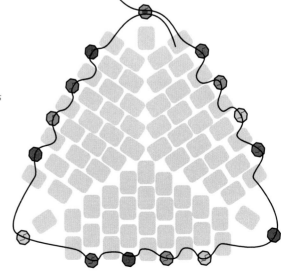

Add the crystals just as you added all the other beads

In a nutshell!
- Increase a triangle up to 5 beads a side
- Add a Point Round and 1 more round using 1 bead in every space
- Bead 4 more rounds with 1 bead in every space, the first round of which uses crystals
- Decrease the triangle until you have 1 bead per side

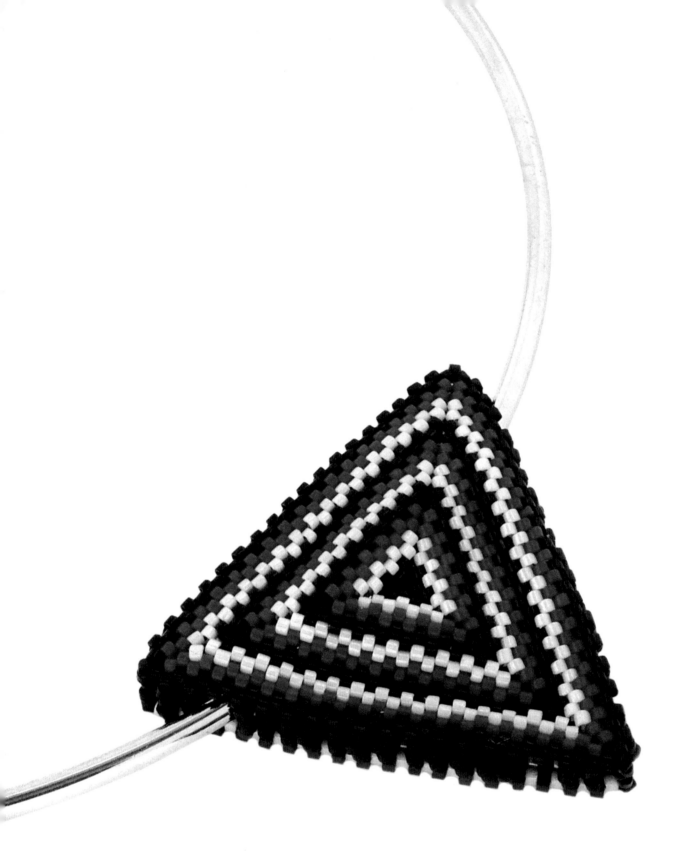

Reversible Triangle Pendant

Two simply beaded triangles easily turn into four different pendants in one...

Simple triangles are an effective design tool as they can be striking, subtle, patterned or plain. When you add another side, and then a clever way of finishing, you end up with 4 different pendants in one – more bang for your beadwork!

Materials
- 5g of size 11 cylinder beads in black – your A beads
- 3g of size 11 cylinder beads in cream – your B beads
- 1.5g of size 11 cylinder beads in red – your C beads

I used
- Black – DB10
- Cream – DB203
- Red – DB791

Variations
- Why not ignore the stripes and just use solid colours? Or dot in a variety of colours depending on what beads you have

Sizing
Continuing increasing until there are a larger number of beads on each side will give you larger triangles

Techniques
- Beading a Triangle, page 28

THE STEPS...

STEP 1
Pick up 3A and join into a circle by threading through the first bead.

STEP 2
Using a Herringbone Increase, add 2A into every gap between the beads added in Step 1.

STEP 3
*Peyote 2B, 1B. Repeat from * twice more to finish the round.

STEP 4
*Peyote 2B, 1B, 1B. Repeat from * twice more to finish the round.

STEP 5
*Peyote 2C, 1C, 1C, 1C. Repeat from * twice more to finish the round.

Step 3

Step 1

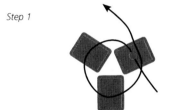

Step 2

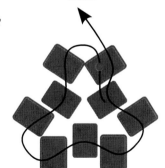

Step 4

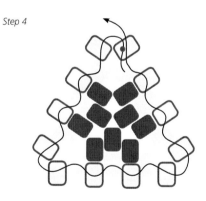

Step 5

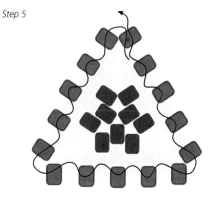

TOP TIP
Pay attention to the joining as you want to ensure you leave holes for threading your pendant onto whatever you choose

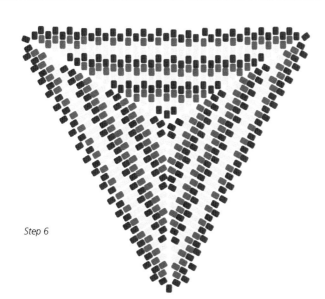

Step 6

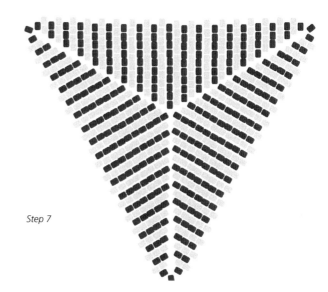

Step 7

STEP 6
Continue adding rounds, for 14 more rounds using the following colours:
C, A, A, B, B, C, C, A, A, B, B, C, C, A, until there are 19 single beads a side. Bead one round using just 1A bead in every space, including the corners.

STEP 7
Repeat steps 1-6 to bead another triangle but only using each colour for one round, starting with 3 B beads, and alternating just B and A rounds. The last round will have only one bead in each space and uses A beads.

STEP 8
Weave to exit one of the corner beads in either triangle. Bring your two triangles together. Pick up 3A beads. Weave through the corner bead in your other piece, making sure you go through it in the opposite direction than your thread is exiting the first bead.

STEP 9
Thread back through the 3 new beads and weave through the first corner on your first piece, entering it from the other side than you exited it. Pull tight.

STEP 10
Weave through your work to be exiting the next edge bead in your first triangle. Do this carefully, making sure that your thread doesn't show and you keep your work tight.

STEP 11
Repeat joining the two triangles with groups of 3 beads until you have filled in all 3 sides. However, always leave the 3rd after each corner, and the 3rd before each corner, empty to allow room to thread the triangles onto your stringing material

Step 8

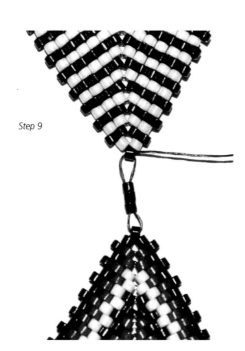

Step 9

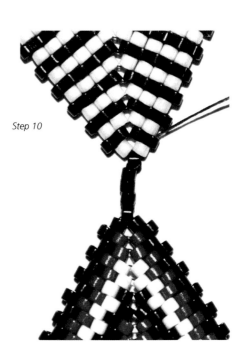

Step 10

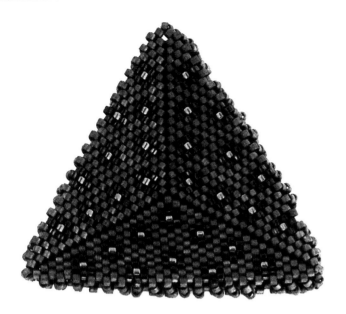

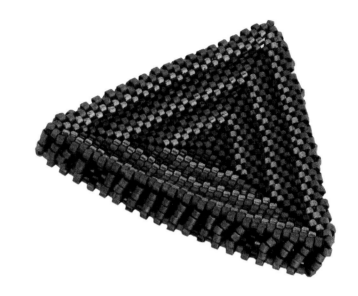

For this more detailed variation Jo Prowse used stripes of DB22L, DB322 and DB4 on one side and then on the other she beaded 'flowers' using her two highlight colours

66 Want to change things up?
Then wear the pendant with one
point facing upwards
for a different look 99

Step 11

This pendant is endlessly variable, depending on your bead stash, taste and mood

For this more advanced variation Jo Prowse used DB1055 with DB1851 dotted on one side and a bolder flower motif on the reverse

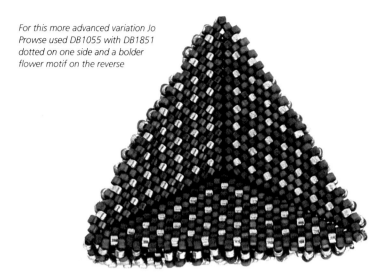
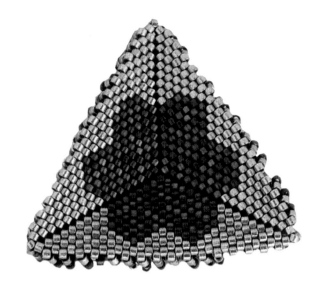

This copper colour variation shows how Jo Prowse used stripes, with DB2, DB322 and DB40 on one side and then dots of colours on the other

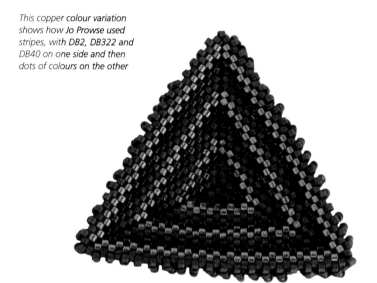
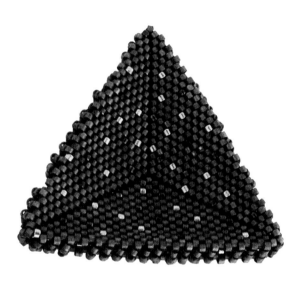

For this variation Jo Prowse used DB871, DB2 and DB1851 to create stripes on one side, with all the increases a single colour, and a diagonal stripe on the other

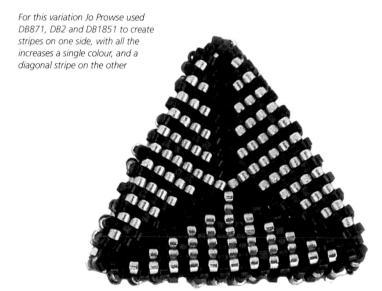

Triangle Beaded Bead

Adding larger central holes to simple beaded beads means you can begin to use them in many other ways

When a beaded bead has a larger central hole it means that your stringing options are increased and you can combine your beadwork with cord, wirework, beaded ropes and much more

Materials
To make one beaded bead in 4 colours
- ½ g size 11 cylinder beads in colour A
- ½ g size 11 cylinder beads in colour B
- ½ g size 11 cylinder beads in colour C
- 3 size 11 cylinder beads in colour D

Variations
If you want to alter the look of your beaded beads then after beading the Point Round, add an even number of rounds of plain circular peyote stitch with 1 bead in every space to add depth to the outside walls of your beaded beads

Colours
- All your beads can be the same colour for solid colour block beaded beads
- Your B, C and D can all be the same
- Your A, C and D can all be the same for outlined shapes on your beaded beads

Techniques
- Beading a Triangle, page 28
- Zipping and Joining, page 22

THE STEPS...
Increasing section

STEP 1
Pick up 12A beads and join them into a circle by threading through the first 2 beads.

> **TOP TIP**
> *This means your tail is in the right place to use later on, or you can use your working thread after Step 8*

STEP 2
Peyote stitch 1A into every space. Make sure you Step-Up to end.

STEP 3
*Peyote stitch 2A, 1B. Repeat from * twice more.

> **TOP TIP**
> *Your central tube needs to be an odd number of rounds if you want your corners to match up*

> **TOP TIP**
> *Be aware that at first you'll be beading a plain tube so make sure you pull this tight – this will reduce any threads which may show otherwise*

> **TOP TIP**
> *Don't forget to Step-Up at the end of every round. When you're increasing this will mean splitting pairs of beads*

This diagram shows the beads you will add for Steps 3–7

STEP 4
*Peyote stitch 2A, 1B, 1B. Repeat from * twice more.

STEP 5
*Peyote stitch 2A, 1B, 1C, 1B. Repeat from * twice more.

STEP 6
*Peyote stitch 2A, 1B, 1C, 1C, 1B. Repeat from * twice more.

STEP 7
Point Round – *Peyote stitch 1A, 1B, 1C, 1D, 1C, 1B. Repeat from * twice more.

Marilyn Norman mixed the colours and textures of beads she used to create these striking beaded beads

In a nutshell!
- Bead an odd number of rounds of circular peyote using a multiple of 6 beads
- Increase as far as you wish
- Bead a Point Round
- Return to the start of your work and bead the same number of increasing rounds, ensuring your corners match up
- Zip the edges of your work together

Step 8

Step 10

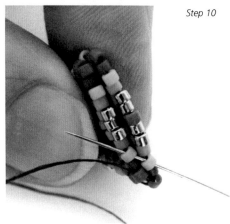

Violetta Pretorius used solid colours to create triangles that combine and can be mixed and matched depending on your mood

Second Side

STEP 8

Thread back to the start of your work. You will thread through 7 beads in a diagonal line.

You are now back to the plain peyote rows at the start of your work and exiting through one of your 'up' beads.

STEP 9

Repeat steps 3–6 to bead the other side. Make sure you Step-Up to end.

STEP 10

The last step is to zip the two sides together by weaving through the Point Round as though you are adding the beads in it to the second side you beaded.

STEP 11

Weave your thread through your work to secure and finish □

Playing around with colours and pattern creates an interesting chain

Turning these triangles into a chain is simply a matter of joining your beads in Step 1 into a circle through another triangle

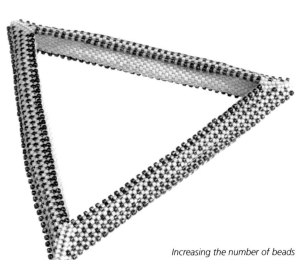

Increasing the number of beads you pick up in Step 1 means you increase the size of the central hole, as in this bangle

Extra Charts
If you want to play around with colour and pattern here are some extra charts for variation

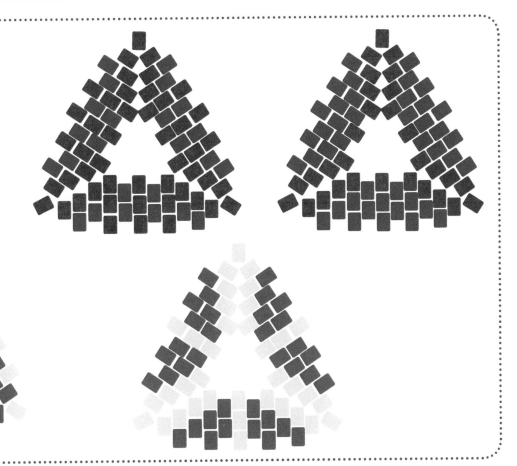

For these I began with 36 beads and then increased until there were 11 beads along each side

Frame Beaded Beads

Triangular beaded beads are great in themselves, but when you play with space you can create beaded frames to highlight your treasures

Adding only some beads in a round means that when you come to zip up your work you can leave spaces, and spaces are perfect for filling with other beads...

Materials
To make one beaded bead
- 1.5g of size 11 seed beads in a mix of colours
- Approximately 20–25 6mm pearls

I used
- A mix of green size 11 seed beads and some copper pearls with a hint of green

Variations
You could use any beads in the centre to decorate the beaded beads. Why not try fire-polished, crystals, rounds...
- Size and shape – simply continuing increasing on each side will give you larger triangles, which could be used to frame larger beads
- You can skip Step 6 and zipping up completely, to have more open frame beads
- Don't stop at beaded beads. Picking up a much larger number of beads to start would give you a frame beaded bangle...

Sizing
You can make these any size you choose – it just depends on what you want to add into the centre

Techniques
- Beading a Triangle, page 28
- Zipping and Joining, page 22

> **TOP TIP**
> *Circling through 4 beads at the start puts your tail thread in the exact place ready for you to use in Step 4*

THE STEPS...
The first side

STEP 1
Pick up 24A beads and circle through the first four to join into a circle. Then add 3 more rounds of circular peyote stitch with 12 beads per round.

STEP 2
Using A beads, increase your triangle until you have 9 beads along a side
(6 rounds of increasing).

> **TOP TIP**
> *What you bead in Step 1 makes a tube, which becomes the threading hole for your bead; it's only after Step 2 that you actually increase.*

STEP 3
Point Round – Bead this round with 1A only in each corner space and the spaces either side of the corners. Every other space will be empty.

In a nutshell!
- Join 24 beads into a circle
- Bead 3 rounds of circular peyote stitch
- Increase until 9 beads a side
- Bead a point round with only beads in the corner spaces and those either side of that
- Return to your tail thread and increase the second side until 9 beads a side
- Fill centre with beads
- Zip edges together

> **TOP TIP**
> *When beading Step 3, make sure you weave through your work to hide the thread for the spaces with no beads in*

Step 2

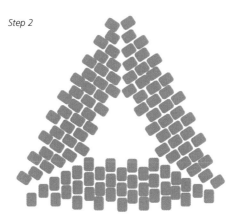

Step 3

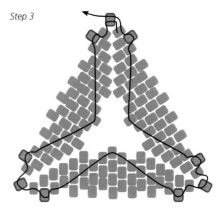

The second side
STEP 4
Return to your tail thread and repeat Step 2 on this edge.

STEP 5
Using a separate piece of thread, add a circle of your feature beads into the frame of the beadwork.

STEP 6
Zip the two edges of your beadwork together using the beads added in Step 3, again making sure to hide your thread as you work ⬜

❝The choices of what you use to fill your frames are endless, let your imagination, and your beads, run wild!❞

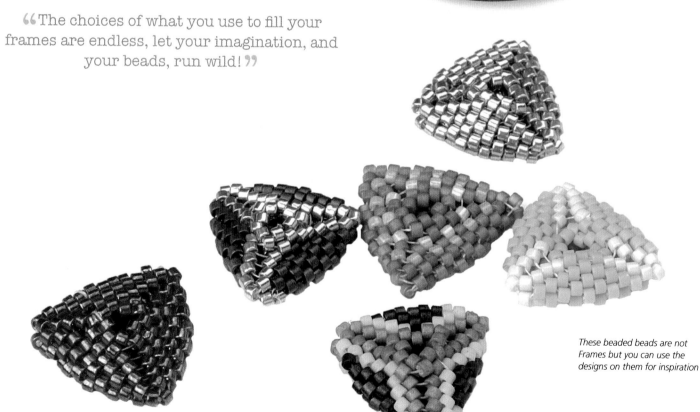

These beaded beads are not Frames but you can use the designs on them for inspiration

*Sanya Preston used bold monochromes to make
beaded beads that frame pearls and crystals*

*Violetta Pretorius made frame
beaded beads to coordinate with
her plain triangle beaded beads*

Beginner Triangle Bangle

The triangle is the simplest of geometric shapes to bead, and this project is a great way to learn a lot of the techniques introduced in this book

Pay attention as you work – these triangles are so small you'll be increasing and decreasing before you know it!

Using one colour of bead and rapid increasing and decreasing makes for an eye-catching piece that works up quickly. Using a bought finding to thread your beadwork onto makes for an unusual look and cuts down your beading time! An added bonus is that this piece can easily be transformed into the centrepiece of a necklace in the blink of an eye

Materials
- 12g of size 11 cylinder beads in copper
- Bangle (or neck) wire where one end unscrews

I used
- Copper – DB40

Sizing
This piece is easy to size as you create its length as you go. But be aware that it's quite firm and as there is no plain peyote between increases and decreases your work won't be as flexible as if there were

Colour advice
I used just one colour for this bangle but the colour options are endless… you could make each triangle a different colour… use two colours and alternate them for a triangle, or even just one side of a triangle… why not use one colour for all the increasing and decreasing ridges?

Techniques
- Beading a Triangle, page 28

THE STEPS…

STEP 1
Pick up 3 beads and circle through the first one to join into a circle.

STEP 2
Herringbone Increase, adding 2 beads in every gap. Step-Up at the end of the round to exit the first bead added; this will mean you splitting a pair of beads.

Step 1

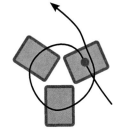

Step 2

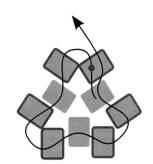

STEP 3
*Peyote 2, 1. Repeat from * twice more to finish the round.

STEP 4
*Peyote 2, 1, 1. Repeat from * twice more to finish the round.

Step 3

Step 4

In a nutshell!
- Bead a triangle increase until you have 4 beads a side
- Bead a Point Round
- Decrease the triangle until you have 2 beads a side
- Repeat increasing and decreasing until it's the size you desire
- Remove starter rounds if needed and thread work onto purchased bangle base

Lynne Faulkner used size 11 seed beads in green to bead her bangle

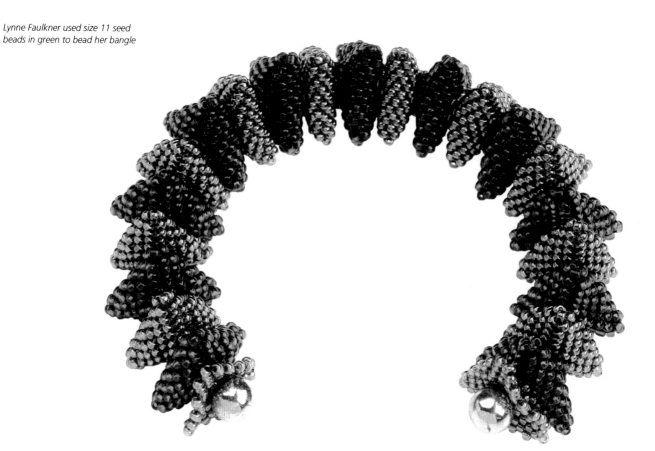

Rebecca Williams used DB164, 177, 862, 920, 1315 and 1763 to make her purple bangle

Step 5
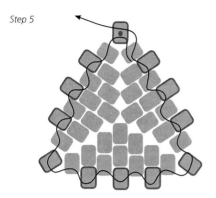

Step 6
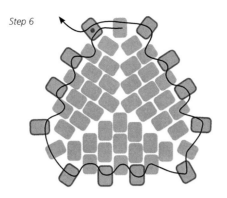

Step 7
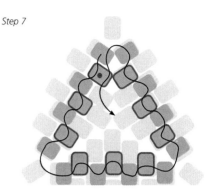

Step 8
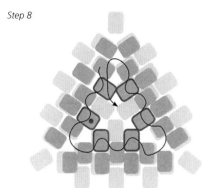

Step 9
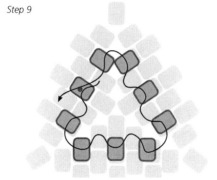

"Altering the size of your triangles is just a matter of increasing for an extra round and adding in an extra decrease to match it"

Step 10 - the hole at the start is enlarged to allow the bangle to be threaded onto the base

STEP 5
Point Round – bead this by stitching 1 bead into every space.

STEP 6
Peyote stitch 1 bead into every space.

STEP 7
Now you'll begin to decrease. *Peyote 1, 1, 1 and nothing in the next space. Repeat from * twice more to finish the round. Step-Up at the end of the round to exit the first bead added.

STEP 8
*Peyote 1A, 1A and nothing in the next space. Repeat from * twice more to finish the round. Step-Up at the end of the round to exit the first bead added.

STEP 9
You are now back at the equivalent of Step 3. Continue peyote stitching with patterns of increasing and decreasing until your bangle is as long as you desire. Finish by ending after Step 8.

STEP 10
Before threading onto your bangle base you may find you need to remove the beads added in the first step so that the hole is large enough ☐

TOP TIP
You may now find it helpful to weave through your work to exit a bead near a corner space. This means that you can follow the next instructions exactly

Try and keep your tension nice and tight

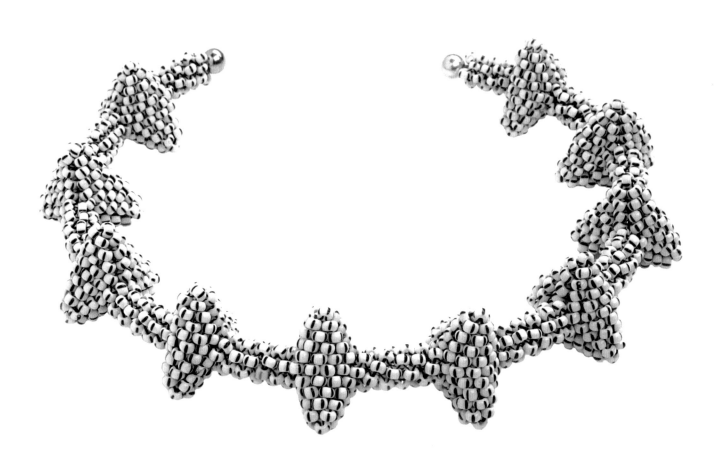

Bold & Beautiful Necklace

Small and intricate not your thing? Then this necklace – speedier to make and dramatic to look at – should be perfect

Using larger beads means you can cut down on your beading time and have something worth showing off much sooner than if you always stuck to the tiny. This necklace also uses a purchased metal neck wire so that you can do away with worrying about a clasp or sizing and make lots of them to have an interchangeable wardrobe of Bold & Beautiful Beadwork

Pay attention as you work – these triangles are big in size but only contain a few rounds, so you'll be increasing and decreasing before you know it!

Materials
- 100g of size 8 seed beads
- 1 metal neck wire with an end that unscrews

I used
- I used white seed beads with a black stripe and then sprinkled in a few with a blue stripe just to keep it interesting

Variations
- Colours – why not change bead colour every few rounds? Make each triangle a different colour?
- Size and shape – simply carrying on increasing and then decreasing the same amount will give you larger triangles.
- If you don't want to use a neck wire you can thread your beadwork onto chain or cord, or bead enough tubular rope to fit over your head

Sizing
The main sizing issue to be aware of is ensuring that your beadwork fits onto your neck wire. You can make your piece long enough to cover the whole wire or as short as you wish

Techniques
- Beading a Triangle, page 28

> **TOP TIP**
> *As you bead, ensure your work is loose enough that it will easily thread onto your neck wire*

THE STEPS...
Rope section
STEP 1
Pick up 6 beads and circle through the first one to join into a circle. Using tubular peyote stitch and just 3 beads per round, add another 10 rounds of beadwork to give you 12 in total.

Step 1

> ### In a nutshell!
> - Bead 12 rounds of circular peyote using 3 beads per round
> - Increase a triangle until 5 beads a side
> - Bead a Point Round
> - Decrease until 1 bead a side
> - Continue beading rope and triangles until the work fits your neck wire or is as long as you desire

Increasing
STEP 2
Using a Herringbone Increase, add 2 beads in every space. Step-Up at the end of the round to exit the first bead added; this will mean you splitting a pair of beads.

STEP 3
*Herringbone Increase 2 beads into the first space and 1 bead into the second. Repeat from * twice more to finish the round.

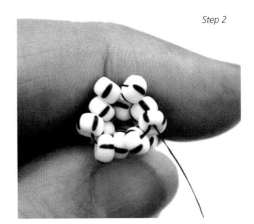
Step 2

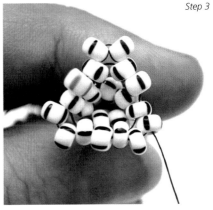
Step 3

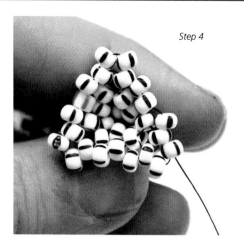

Step 4

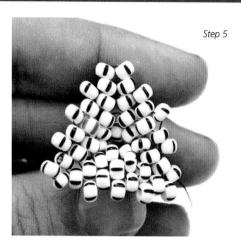

Step 5

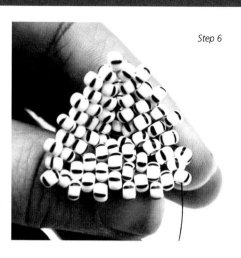

Step 6

STEP 4

*Herringbone Increase 2 beads into the first space and 1 bead into the next two. Repeat from * twice more to finish the round.

STEP 5

*Herringbone Increase 2 beads into the first space and 1 bead into the next three. Repeat from * twice more to finish the round.

STEP 6
Point Round
Peyote stitch 1 bead into every space.

Marie New used 4 different coloured seed beads (frosted green – A, blue – B, pinky-cream – C and metallic blue – D) to bead this patterned variation. Right at the start she picked up alternate A and B beads to give her rope a stripe, which she continued throughout the piece. Then for the triangles she used C beads for the last round of the rope and the first 3 rounds of increasing, then switched to D beads for 2 rounds then back to C for 4 rounds. For her next triangle she swapped over her C and D beads and continued alternating them for the rest of the necklace

Decreasing

STEP 7
Peyote stitch 1 bead into every space.

STEP 8
*Peyote 1 bead into the next 4 spaces and nothing in the fifth, which is the corner. Repeat from * twice more to finish the round. Step-Up at the end of the round to exit the first bead added.

STEP 9
*Peyote 1 bead into the next 3 spaces and nothing in the fourth. Repeat from * twice more to finish the round. Step-Up at the end of the round to exit the first bead added.

STEP 10
*Peyote 1 bead into the next 2 spaces and nothing in the third. Repeat from * twice more to finish the round. Step-Up at the end of the round to exit the first bead added.

STEP 11
*Peyote 1 bead into the next space and nothing in the second. Repeat from * twice more to finish the round. Step-Up at the end of the round to exit the first bead added.

STEP 12
Using tubular peyote stitch and just 3 beads per round (1 in each corner space) add 12 rounds of beadwork. You may find it helpful to count out 36 beads before you start.

STEP 13
Return to Step 2 and begin increasing again. Continue peyote stitching with patterns of increasing and decreasing until you have added a total of 10 triangles. Finish your work with 12 rounds of tubular peyote stitch. Thread your work onto your neck wire and wear with pride! □

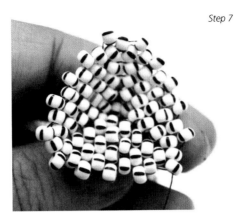
Step 7

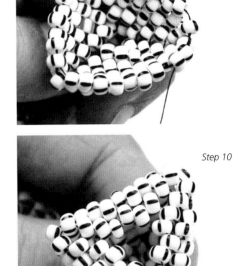
Step 8

Step 9

Step 10

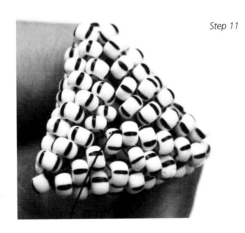
Step 11

Step 12

WANT SOMETHING MORE SUBTLE?
"Then the same necklace can be beaded using size 11 seed or cylinder beads"

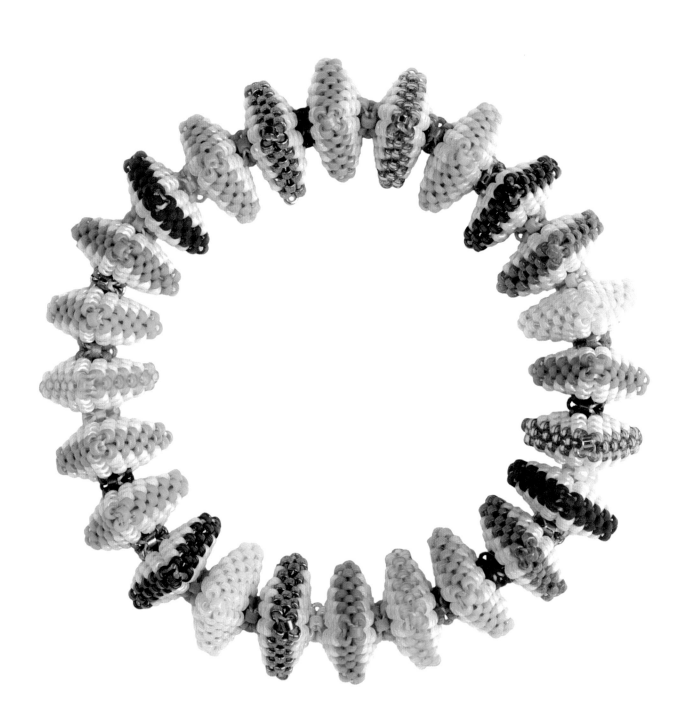

Beginner Power Puff

Small triangles, basic colour changes and the addition of zipping your work add up to a great way to learn the core techniques of geometric beading and assembling finished pieces. Once you've mastered the steps you can move onto experimenting with one of the many possible variations

Materials
- 7g of size 11 cylinder beads in a cream – your A beads
- 7g of size 11 cylinder beads in other colours (I used a mix of 12 different colours) – your B beads

I used
- Cream – DB203
- Colours – a complete mix of ends of tubes and what I found hidden under my bead mat

Variations
- Colours – Why not have all your beads the same? Or your A and B beads could just be two colours for a more monochrome look
- Size and shape – Simply repeating the principles of steps 5 and 8 will give you large triangles. Repeating steps 6 and 7 gives you wider triangles
- Beaded beads – Beading Steps 1–11 will give you a simple beaded bead

Techniques
- Beading a Triangle, page 28
- Zipping and Joining, page 22

Sizing
This piece is easy to size as you create its length as you go. But be aware that it's quite floppy and so you may need to bead it shorter than you usually would

THE STEPS...

STEP 1
Pick up 3B beads and circle through the first one to join into a circle.

STEP 2
Herringbone Increase using 2A in every space. Step-Up at the end of the round to exit the first bead added; this will mean splitting a pair of beads.

STEP 3
*Herringbone Increase 2A, peyote 1A. Repeat from * twice more to finish the round.

STEP 4
*Herringbone Increase 2A, peyote 1A, 1A. Repeat from * twice more to finish the round.

Step 1

Step 2

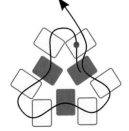

Step 3

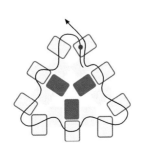

Step 4

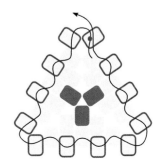

In a nutshell!
- Bead a triangle increase until you have 5 beads a side
- Bead a Point Round
- Decrease the triangle until you have 2 beads a side
- Bead 3 plain rounds of tubular peyote
- Repeat increasing and decreasing until it's the size you desire
- Zip the ends together

Step 5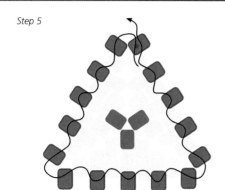

Step 7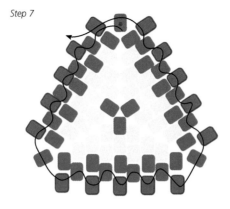

Step 9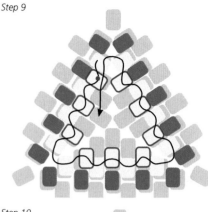

Step 6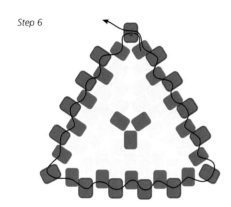

Step 8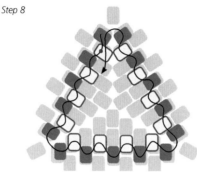

Step 10

STEP 5
*Herringbone Increase 2B, peyote 1B, 1B, 1B. Repeat from * twice more to finish the round.

STEP 6
Point Round – Bead this by stitching 1B into every space.

STEP 7
Peyote stitch 1B into every space.

STEP 8
Now you'll begin to decrease. *Peyote 1A, 1A, 1A, 1A and nothing in the next space. Repeat from * twice more to finish the round. Step-Up at the end of the round to exit the first bead added.

STEP 9
*Peyote 1A, 1A, 1A and nothing in the next space. Repeat from * twice more to finish the round. Step-Up at the end of the round to exit the first bead added.

STEP 10
*Peyote 1A, 1A and nothing in the next space. Repeat from * twice more to finish the round. Step-Up at the end of the round to exit the first bead added.

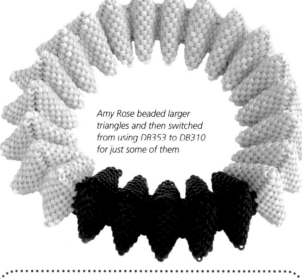

Amy Rose beaded larger triangles and then switched from using DB353 to DB310 for just some of them

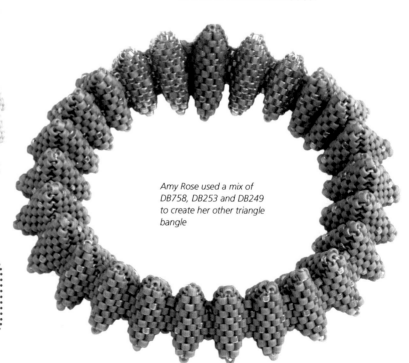

Amy Rose used a mix of DB758, DB253 and DB249 to create her other triangle bangle

Colour advice
This bracelet uses at least 2 colours, which makes it easier to see what you're doing, but feel free to use just one or as many as you desire

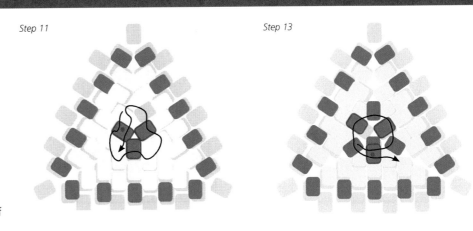

Step 11

Step 13

STEP 11
Peyote stitch 1B in every space.

STEP 12
Peyote stitch 1B in every space.

STEP 13
Peyote stitch 1B in every space.

STEP 14
You are now back at the equivalent of Step 2. Continue peyote stitching with patterns of increasing and decreasing until your bangle is as long as you desire.

STEP 15
You are now ready to zip the ends together. I find it easier to do this not in a valley after decreasing, but instead undo the start of my work, removing the beads added in Steps 1–5 (I know I have removed enough when I have a round with one bead in each corner rather than two). I then bead the end of my work up to Step 4 and use the beads at the start to replicate adding Step 5 ▫

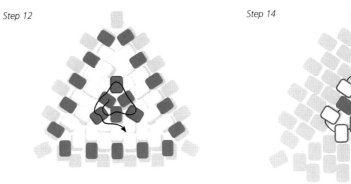

Step 12

Step 14

Colour advice
I used a mix of different colours for my B beads, changing colour each time I came to a section using Bs but keeping the same colour for that section

Step 15

Dee Wingrove-Smith beaded her bangle using DB1132 and 1134 and added a popper fastener instead of zipping the ends together

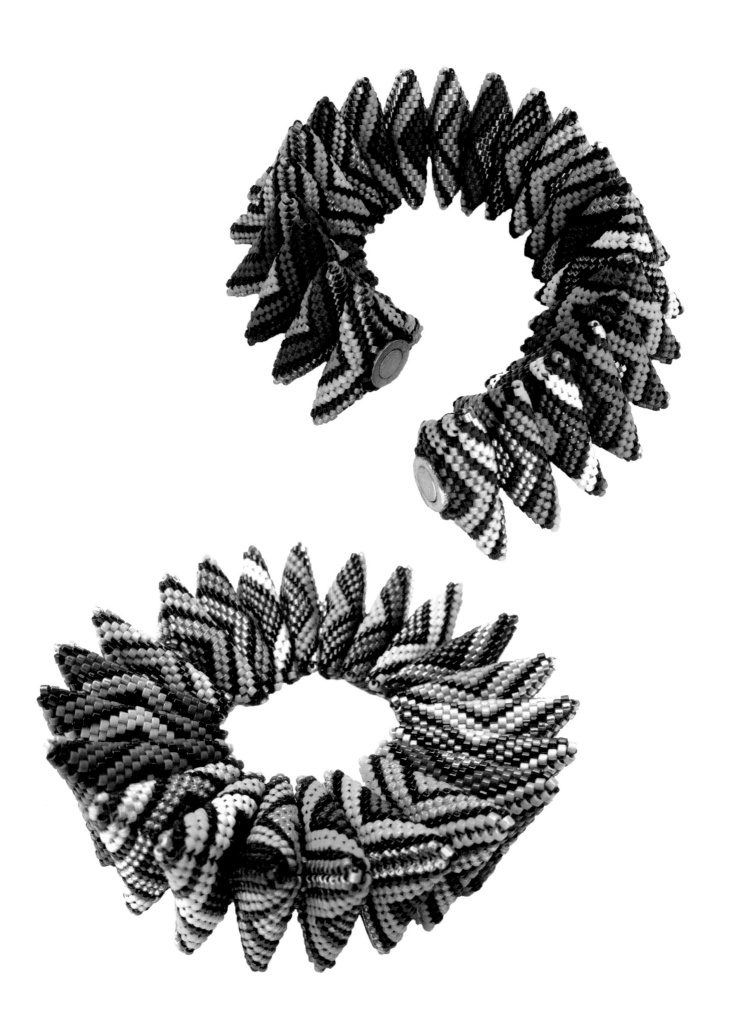

Caldera Bangle

Go colour crazy with this dramatic bangle using basic triangle increasing and decreasing but adding in a pattern for an advanced step

For this bangle, I chose a black stripe, and then went wild in my bead stash and used over 70 different colours to fill in. This is the perfect piece to use small quantities of beads you've been saving, want to try in a piece, or have left over from other projects

Clasp
If you want to add a clasp to your work, such as Carla Engelman did using a magnetic clasp on her Caldera at the top of the main photo (or as Dee Wingrove-Smith did with a popper fastener for her bangle on page 59), then stitch one in either when you have decreased right down or partially down, depending on what you're using

Materials
- 8–10g of size 11 cylinder beads for the stripe – your A beads
- 40–42g size 11 cylinder beads for the colour fields

I used
- Stripe – DB10
- Colours – All Miyuki size 11 Delicas (some were not labelled, so not all I used are here): 60, 76, 135, 149, 174, 177, 190, 210, 216, 239, 264, 265, 277, 285, 361, 371, 373, 374, 375, 376, 378, 432, 627, 654, 658, 659, 660, 661, 685, 691, 682, 707, 725, 370, 733, 746, 748, 754, 759, 760, 783, 786, 792, 798, 799, 878, 881, 1052, 1054, 1209, 1250, 1284, 1304, 1341, 1363, 1376, 1536, 1566, 1578, 1769, 1850

Techniques
- Beading a Triangle, page 28
- Zipping and Joining, page 22

In a nutshell!
- Using triangle increasing, bead a triangle using the set pattern until it has 11 beads along a side
- Bead a Point Round
- Decrease until you have 3 beads a side
- Continue increasing and decreasing until the bangle is the length you require
- Zip the ends together

THE STEPS...
Increasing section
STEP 1
Thread your beading needle with a comfortable length of thread and pick up 3A beads. Circle through the first one to join the beads into a circle.

STEP 2
Using Herringbone Increases, add 2B beads in each space. This addition of six beads will complete the second round, and you can see that now you have both corners and sides.

STEP 3
*Herringbone Increase using 2B and peyote 1A. Repeat from * twice more to finish the round.

STEP 4
* Herringbone Increase using 2B and peyote 1A and 1A. Repeat from * twice more to finish the round.

STEP 5
* Herringbone Increase using 2B and peyote 1A, 1C and 1A. Repeat from * twice more to finish the round.

Step 1

Step 2

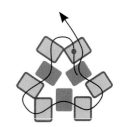

Step 3

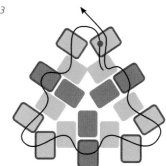

Step 4

Step 5

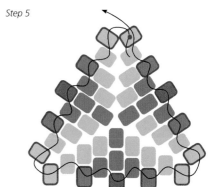

Step 6

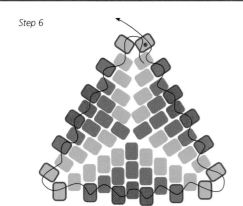

Step 7

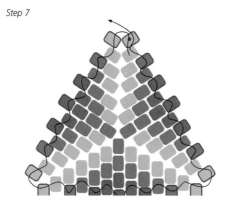

Step 8

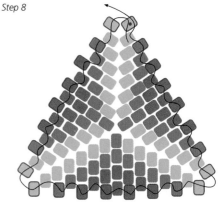

Step 9

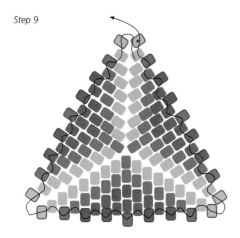

Step 10

Step 11

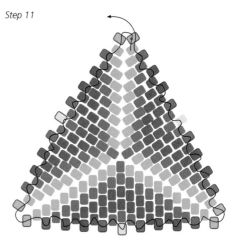

STEP 6
* Herringbone Increase using 2B and peyote 1A, 1C, 1C and 1A. Repeat from * twice more to finish the round.

STEP 7
* Herringbone Increase using 2B and peyote 1A, 1C, 1C, 1C and 1A. Repeat from * twice more to finish the round.

STEP 8
* Herringbone Increase using 2B and peyote 1A, 1C, 1C, 1C, 1C and 1A. Repeat from * twice more to finish the round.

STEP 9
* Herringbone Increase using 2B and peyote 1A, 1C, 1C, 1A, 1C, 1C and 1A. Repeat from * twice more to finish the round.

STEP 10
* Herringbone Increase using 2B and peyote 1A, 1C, 1C, 1A, 1A, 1C, 1C and 1A. Repeat from * twice more to finish the round.

STEP 11
* Herringbone Increase using 2B and peyote 1A, 1C, 1C, 1A, 1D, 1A, 1C, 1C and 1A. Repeat from * twice more to finish the round. This is the last round of increasing.

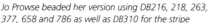

Jo Prowse beaded her version using DB216, 218, 263, 377, 658 and 786 as well as DB310 for the stripe

AJ Reardon used a white/cream stripe with a mix of greens for this fresh version

> **TOP TIP**
> *Note that the colours for the Caldera Bangle will be referred to as A, B, C, D, E, etc. in the instructions, so that you know when to change colour if needed. If you are using just one or a few colours, then repeat them as appropriate*
>
> *Once you have the basic pattern started it becomes easy to see what colour you add where, but until then, pay close attention to the instructions to stay on target*

Step 12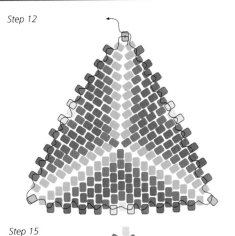

Step 13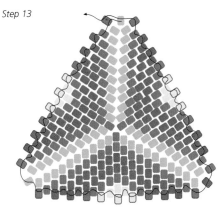

Step 14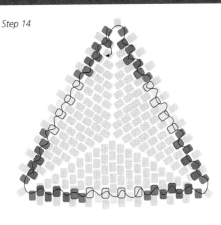

Step 15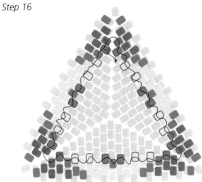

Step 16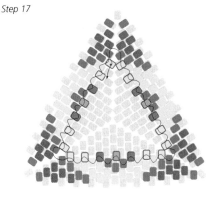

Step 17

STEP 12
Point Round
*Peyote stitch using 1B, 1A, 1C, 1C, 1A, 1D, 1D, 1A, 1C, 1C and 1A. Repeat from * twice more to finish the round.

> **TOP TIP**
> It sounds like more work to take beads out than to join in a valley, but the removal step is much quicker and easier

Decreasing
You now need to pull your work nice and tight as you decrease, so that the form pulls together into a taut shape.
As you are decreasing, and will now be pulling together your corners instead of adding them, you must be extra mindful of your pattern.

STEP 13
*Peyote stitch using 1A, 1C, 1C, 1A, 1D, 1D, 1D, 1A, 1C, 1C and 1A. Repeat from * twice more to finish the round.

STEP 14
*Peyote stitch using 1C, 1C, 1A, 1D, 1D, 1D, 1D, 1A, 1C, 1C and nothing in the corner space. Simply pass your needle through the existing 'corner' beads to bring the sides together. Repeat from * twice more to finish the round.

The diagrams are now showing previous rounds (which are now officially on the other side of the piece) in shadow, to make it clearer for you to see how the new rounds you are adding relate to the other half of your form.

STEP 15
*Peyote stitch using 1C, 1A, 1D, 1D, 1A, 1D, 1D, 1A, 1C and nothing in the corner space. Repeat from * twice more to finish the round.

STEP 16
*Peyote stitch using 1A, 1D, 1D, 1A, 1A, 1D, 1D, 1A and nothing in the corner space. Repeat from * twice more to finish the round.

STEP 17
*Peyote stitch using 1D, 1D, 1A, 1E, 1A, 1D, 1D and nothing in the corner space. Repeat from * twice more to finish the round. Your form should be holding its own now, and behaving like a puff. If not, you aren't pulling it tight enough

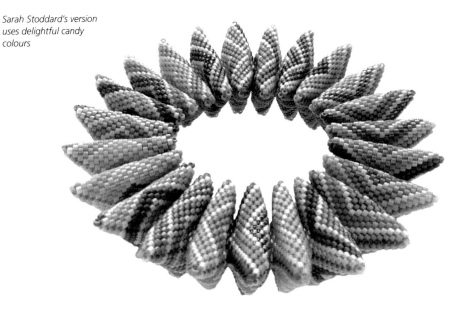

Sarah Stoddard's version uses delightful candy colours

Step 18

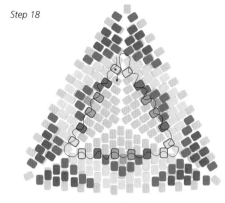

Step 19

Step 20

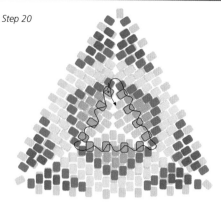

Step 21

Step 22

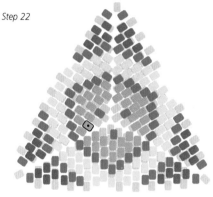

Step 23

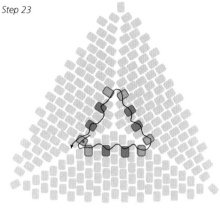

STEP 18
*Peyote stitch using 1D, 1A, 1E, 1E, 1A, 1D and nothing in the corner space. Repeat from * twice more to finish the round.

STEP 19
*Peyote stitch using 1A, 1E, 1E, 1E, 1A and nothing in the corner space. Repeat from * twice more to finish the round.

STEP 20
*Peyote stitch using 1E, 1E, 1E, 1E and nothing in the corner space. Repeat from * twice more to finish the round.

STEP 21
*Peyote stitch using 1E, 1A, 1E, and nothing in the corner space. Repeat from * twice more to finish the round. You are now ready to increase again.

STEP 22
(Optional) If you are just learning this technique or pattern, you might want to move your needle through your work to come out of the second E bead in this round (the outlined bead in the diagram). That way, your starting position on the second puff will match your start on the first one. This can make it easier to follow the pattern.

STEP 23
This step is the same as Step 4, so repeat from that point, but please note that the bead you will be picking up is not a B bead, but an E. From now on it's your choice whether to add in or repeat colours. Continue peyote stitching with patterns of increase and decrease until your bangle is as long as you desire.
   (When you reach the end, if you want your colours to match, you need to be sure that the E in Step 17 onwards is the same as the B bead you used at the start.)

Finishing your work
You are now ready to zip the ends together.
STEP 24
Undo the start of your work, removing the beads added in steps 1–11 (all those up to the Point Round, that is. You'll know you've removed enough when you have a round with one bead in each corner rather than two.) Then bead the end of the work up to Step 11 and use the beads at the start to replicate adding step 12 □

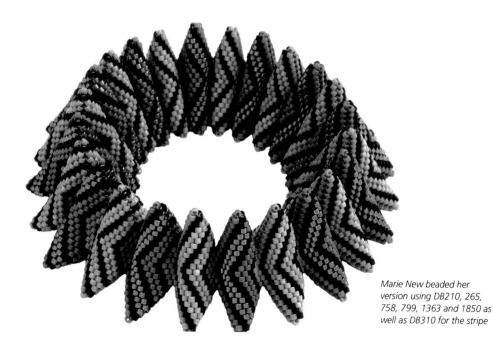

Marie New beaded her version using DB210, 265, 758, 799, 1363 and 1850 as well as DB310 for the stripe

Designing Your Own Power Puff

How to design your own variation...

Playing with a Power Puff is simply a matter of considering, before you begin each round, which direction you want to go in:

- **Do you want to increase?**
  Add 2 beads into where you want the increase to happen

- **Do you want to stay steady?**
  Add 1 bead into each space

- **Do you want to decrease?**
  Add zero beads into where you want the decrease to sit

1. *Increasing and decreasing the same amount each time will give you equal sections on your Power Puff*

2. *Want extra space along an outside edge to add pattern? Then after you've beaded your Point Round add extra rounds of regular circular peyote stitch with 1 bead in every space*

3. *Don't want to go down so far? Just bead fewer decreasing rounds before you increase again*

4. *Want extra height sometimes? Simply increase more. Note that to get you back down to the same point you'll then need to bead more decrease rounds too – but that's optional*

5. *Want extra 'rope' between sections? After you've decreased just bead even-count peyote with 1 bead in every space for as long as you want. Note that if you want your corners to match up every time you'll need to bead an even number of rounds*

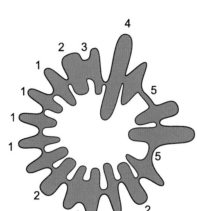

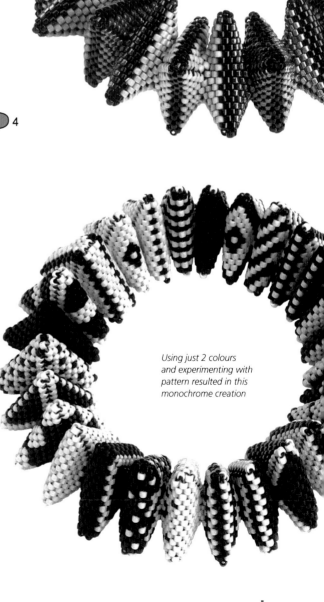

Instead of lining up your triangles so the corners match, why not play around with their placement for a spikier creation?

Using just 2 colours and experimenting with pattern resulted in this monochrome creation

Using extra plain rounds of peyote after increasing and before decreasing gives you 'sides' to your triangles which are perfect for adding pattern to, as in this black, white and red bangle

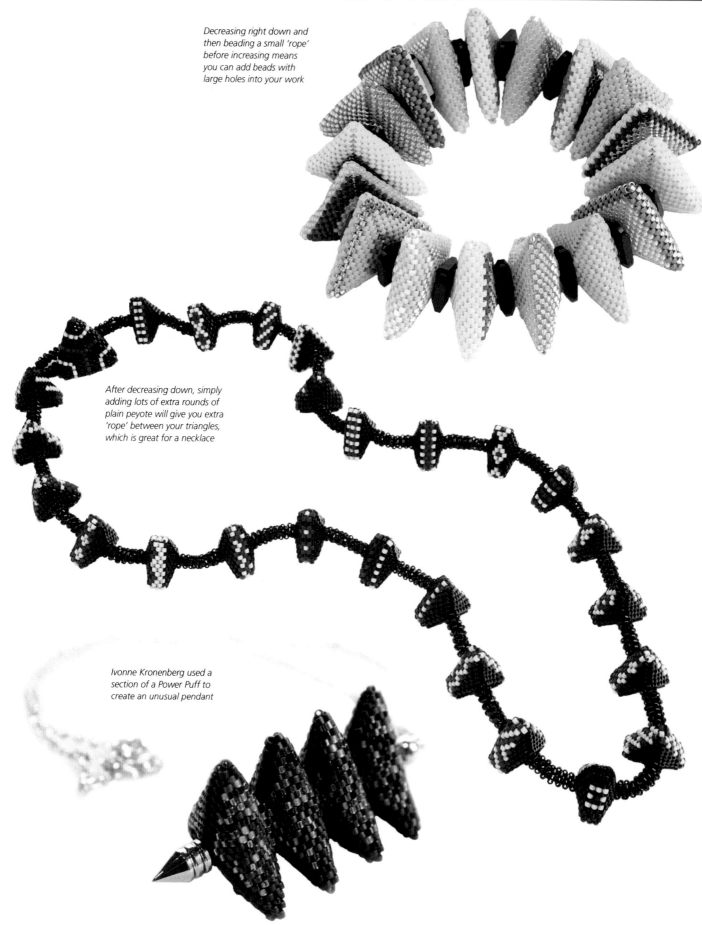

Decreasing right down and then beading a small 'rope' before increasing means you can add beads with large holes into your work

After decreasing down, simply adding lots of extra rounds of plain peyote will give you extra 'rope' between your triangles, which is great for a necklace

Ivonne Kronenberg used a section of a Power Puff to create an unusual pendant

Lia Melia beaded her Power Puffs using tiny size 15 cylinder beads!

Janet Rosenberg used zingy colours mixed with a translucent cream for this dynamic variation

Kate McKinnon's Power Puff is a delight of colour!

Jeannine Lescure Rainone made individual little puffs with drops on their points

Open holes in Power Puffs
Want to add something extra to your Power Puff?

Power Puffs can be hung in many different ways; adding 'holes' to them gives you much more flexibility for using, and adds extra interest

> **TOP TIP**
> **FOR ADDING THE HOLES**
> *I like to add the holes on the last triangle of my piece. I bead one side of it at one end and then return to the start and bead the other side of the hole, zipping them to join*
>
> *You can make these holes when you decrease but I find them a lot fiddlier so stick to increasing the two sides to make them*

THE PRINCIPLE...
STEP 1
Bead your triangle as large as desired.

STEP 2
First round adding the hole - Perform a Peyote Decrease in the first corner, and then bead the rest of the round as normal. At the end you'll need to Step-Up into the first bead added.

STEP 3
Bead another round, beginning as normal, but when you come to the last corner add no beads into it and ensure you again Step-Up to exit the first bead added in this round.

STEP 4
Add as many rounds in this manner as you desire (I added an extra 2) until you want to stop the hole. Remember every time that you need to finish your round by weaving through your work to Step-Up into the first bead added.

Then pick up all the beads you need to turn it back into a triangle: this is 4 for every round you didn't add anything in the corner, plus 2 more. So:

- If you missed 1 round - add 6 beads
- If you missed 2 rounds - add 10 beads
- If you missed 3 rounds - add 14 beads
- If you missed 4 rounds - add 18 beads
- If you missed 5 rounds - add 22 beads
- If you missed 6 rounds - add 26 beads

I missed 4 rounds so picked up 18 beads

STEP 5
You can now carry on beading your triangle as before, using the beads added in Step 4 as though they were always there, remembering to bead a Herringbone Increase where the corner should sit.
Herringbone Increases
Your Herringbone Increase will sit after you have beaded as many single peyote stitches as rounds you missed adding beads in (so in my example 4 single beads)

> *❝Power Puffs make great pendants but the addition of a hanging hole makes them much more usable❞*

Step 4

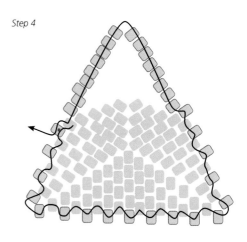

Step 1 *Step 2* *Step 3*

Step 5

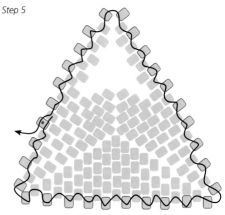

In a nutshell!
- Increase a triangle until 10 beads a side. Add a Point Round
- Decrease until 2 beads a side and then increase again
- Bead 10 triangles in this way
- *Increase for your 11th triangle, beginning to add a hole when you have 3 beads a side and missing adding corner beads for 5 rounds
- Bead your next round adding 22 beads in the corner with the hole
- Bead 2 rounds as you would regularly; add a Point Round
- Return to the beginning of your work and bead the other side of the last triangle as from * above but without the Point Round
- Zip the edges together to complete

Power Puff Ring
Just one Power Puff is ideal to adorn your hand

You can make this ring as bold or subtle as you desire. Play with size, colour and pattern for a whole range of rings

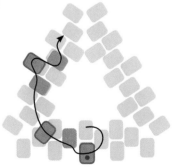

The ring shank is a simple band of peyote stitch zipped onto the other side of your work once beaded

Materials
• 5g of size 11 cylinder beads

Variations
How big you make your ring is entirely up to you – have fun experimenting with different sizes for different looks

Techniques used
• Beading a Triangle, page 28
• Zipping and Joining, page 22

THE STEPS...
STEP 1
Bead a triangle as large as you desire and then decrease down as far as you desire. For the ring in the photos I increased up to 17 beads per side.

STEP 2
Work out how many spaces you have in the next round (this is the number of beads you were going to add per side in this round times 3, i.e. 2 beads per side gives you 6 beads in the circle). Use basic peyote stitch to add 1 bead into half of the number of spaces you just calculated. In the diagrams my ring shank beads are pink.

STEP 3
Change direction and bead peyote stitch again with 1 bead in each of the same number of spaces.

STEP 4
It will take a couple of rows but this will turn into a band – I promise! Continue this pattern of peyote stitch until you have added an even number of rows and the band will fit over your finger.
Zip your last row to the spaces on the other side of your triangle base to complete the ring □

TOP TIP
The amount of beads per side you decrease down to will determine half the width of your ring shank, i.e. 3 beads per side will give you a ring shank 6 beads wide

In a nutshell!
• Bead a triangle increase until it is as large as you wish
• Bead a Point Round
• Decrease the triangle as much as you wish
• Bead a number of plain rows of peyote as wide as you desire
• Zip the ends to turn into a ring

Step 2

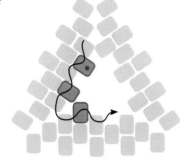

Step 3

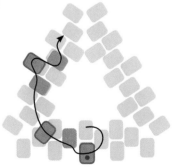

Step 4

Squares

Four sides with a distortion leading to
a world of 3-dimensional possibilities...

Beading a Distorted Square

This book makes use of a specific type of square, which I have called the 'Distorted Square', named simply because it doesn't want to lie flat

A Distorted Square is the perfect example of never giving up. When I was first learning how to bead geometric shapes I spent hours and hours trying to perfect a square and although I beaded it just like I did a triangle it just wouldn't work for me - no matter how flat I tried to make the pieces they kept distorting. Not one to give up, I was determined to get something usable out of these funny little pieces and with a bit of zipping the beaded Jacks and then the Stars appeared. The moral of the story is never give up and never be disheartened if your work doesn't immediately work out as you wish - it may grow into something even better!

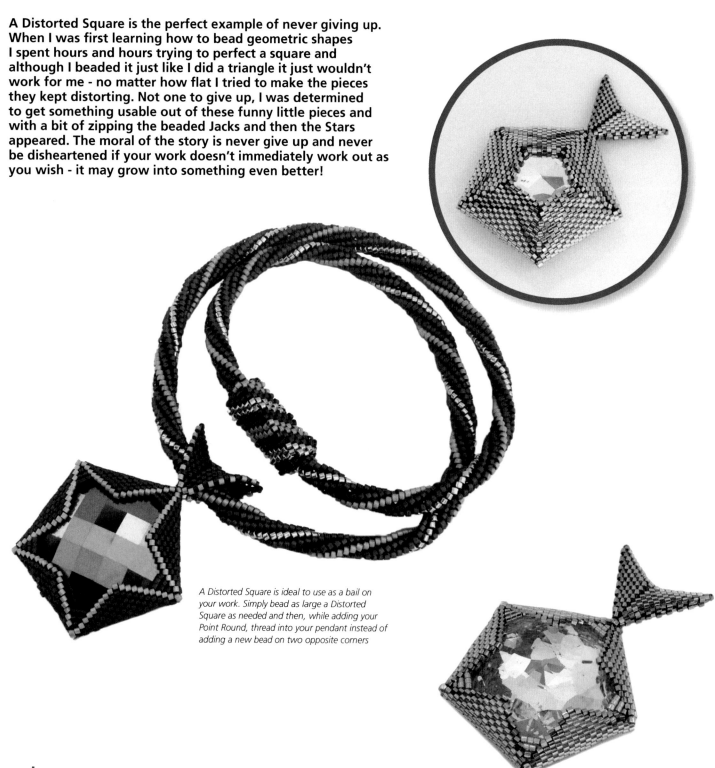

A Distorted Square is ideal to use as a bail on your work. Simply bead as large a Distorted Square as needed and then, while adding your Point Round, thread into your pendant instead of adding a new bead on two opposite corners

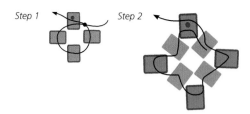 *Step 1* *Step 2*

 *Step 3*

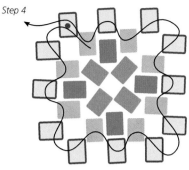 *Step 4*

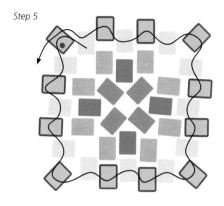 *Step 5*

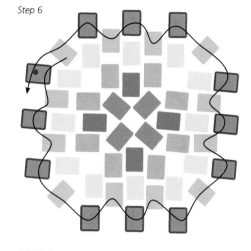 *Step 6*

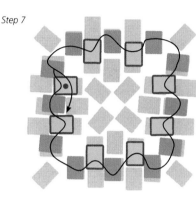 *Step 7*

THE STEPS...
Starting a basic Distorted Square from 4 beads
STEP 1
Join 4 beads into a circle and tie with a knot to hold them extra tight right from the get go. Thread through the next bead along to be in the correct place to continue.

> **TOP TIP**
> *As you bead the square make sure you resist all temptation to push it flat. The tighter you pull it, and the more you let it distort, the tighter the tension in your finished piece.*

> **TOP TIP**
> *Tying a knot right at the start of your work holds your square too tight and helps it to distort, the opposite of what you usually want with your beadwork*

STEP 2
Add 1 bead between each bead in round 1.

STEP 3
Using a Herringbone Increase, add 2 beads into each space. This forms the corners. Make sure at the end of the round you Step-Up to exit the first bead of the first pair you added.

STEP 4
Using a Herringbone Increase, add 2 beads into each corner and 1 bead in every side space.

STEP 5
Repeat Step 4 for as long as you desire (noting that you have 1 extra side space added per side per round), then add a Point Round with 1 bead in every space.

Decreasing a Distorted Square
STEP 6
To decrease a Distorted Square you want to use a Peyote Decrease, so, as with all decreasing, you first need to bead the round with 1 bead in every space so that you end up with beads either side of the corner spaces.

> **TOP TIP**
> *It's very easy to miss the Step-Up and not bead the end of your round as shown in the diagrams. It looks obvious here but it won't be so obvious in your actual work. If you do miss your Step-Up, one side of your square will be smaller than the others and your pieces will never be able to zip together. To help keep track of where you are, why not separate out 8 beads at the start of each round and only take from this pile when you add corners? When you pick up the last 2 you know you're approaching a Step-Up. If you go to bead a corner but have no beads left in your corner pile then check you did your Step-Up*

STEP 7
Bead another round of peyote stitch, but bead a Peyote Decrease on the corner without adding a bead. The beads in your previous round will pull into the centre - but this can take a few rounds until it sits comfortably. Continue this method of decreasing as long as you desire ☐

Distorted Square Beaded Beads

A distorted square is perfect for turning into a beaded bead

Distorted Squares have so many uses. This project shows what happens when you increase and then decrease them to create beaded beads

Above: Barbara Johnson made her beaded beads using blacks and silver for a monochrome look and dotted in beads whenever she desired

Materials
To make one beaded bead
- 1.5g of Size 11 cylinder beads - your A beads
- Beading needle and thread

Variations
- Why not make each side a different colour, play with stripes, add extra plain rounds to give you more depth…
- If you don't like decreasing then don't worry, simply increase a distorted square, then add a Point Round. Bead another square the same size and zip to the Point Round
- If you want to add more depth to the outside edges of these beads then after your Point Round bead an odd-number of plain rounds of circular peyote with 1 bead in every space
- If you want a larger centre to thread through then begin with a number of beads that's a multiple of 4 and bead a small circular peyote tube before increasing

Using the beads
These beaded beads can be worn by threading a jump ring through one of the corner beads and hanging like charms or by threading through the hole created by the 4 beads at the start

Techniques
- Beading a Distorted Square, page 74

TOP TIP
Remember to let your work distort if you want a really different look

THE STEPS…
Increasing section
STEP 1
Pick up 4A beads and circle through the first four to join into a circle

STEP 2
Peyote stitch 1A into every space.

STEP 3
Using a Herringbone Increase, add 2A into every space. Step up at the end of the round to exit the first bead added.

STEP 4
Continue increasing your Distorted Square until you have 7 beads along each side.

STEP 5
Point Round- Add 1 bead into every space.

STEP 6
Adding width to your beaded beads- Bead a further three rounds with 1 bead in every space. You can add more rounds if desired as long as you add an odd total of rounds and end with a single bead either side of the corner spaces.

STEP 7
Using the basic decreasing instructions decrease your work by adding nothing into the corner spaces until you have decreased down to just 1 bead a side. Weave through these last 4 beads to finish ☐

Step 4

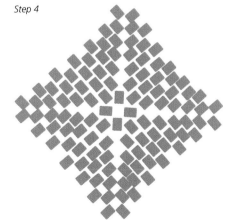

Step 5

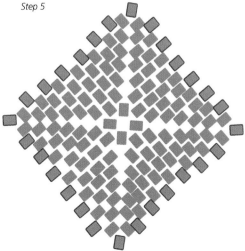

In a nutshell!
- Increase a Distorted Square as much as you choose
- Bead a Point Round
- Decrease the square until back at 4 beads

Joining Squares

These beaded pieces are perfect for joining into double-sided beads, Jacks or Stars. The principles of making them all are the same - the only difference is how many pieces you join

Corners

When joining two pieces together use the beads in the Point Round of one piece as though they were new beads and 'add' them to the second piece
The main thing you need to be aware of is adding extra beads in the correct places

When zipping to make Jacks or Stars you ALWAYS need to add new beads in the corners which sit at the centre front or back of the piece

However, for the corners which sit on the outside points, if there is a corner bead already there then you 'share' it rather than adding a new one

The corners which sit at the centre front and back always need new beads added

The corners on the outside points only need new beads if there is not one already there. If there is one then you thread through it

The principle of joining

- Your first piece always has the Point Round added (this is for the next piece to join onto)
- Your second piece is zipped to the first along two sides and then has its Point Round beads filled in on the last two sides. (This is to give your third piece the beads to join onto)
- Your third and subsequent pieces are joined as the second, except for the final piece, which joins onto the last piece added and the first piece and only needs 2 new beads - in the centre front and back corners

Where to start

I recommend beginning by beading a distorted square, with a Point Round, and then bead another without a Point Round and join it to the first. This will give you all the basics needed to continue.

Joining pieces

Chose what you want to make: 3 or 4 pieces make a jack, 5 or 6 make a star. These instructions assume you're joining 3 or more.

THE STEPS...

STEP 1
Bead the first of your Distorted Squares, including the Point Round.

STEP 2
Bead a second Distorted Square, without a Point Round but otherwise the same size.

STEP 3
Zip the second square to the first:

A - In the first 3 diagrams the yellow beads are those which you will use to zip your pieces together. The blue beads are any new ones you will add.

Begin by picking up 1 corner bead. Ensure this is one of the corners which will sit at the front or back of the Star or Jack you're making, not at the outside corner points.

B - Weave between your two squares, but instead of adding new beads, use the beads in the Point Round of your first piece. Zip this along one side, around one corner and along the next side.

C - Add a new bead for the third corner and then the rest of the Point Round of your second piece until you are back at the start again. If only joining 3 pieces then jump to Step 5

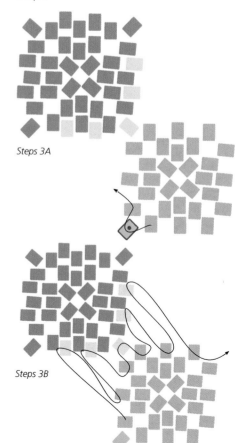

Steps 3A

Steps 3B

STEP 4
Bead the third square and join it to the second as you joined the first two. Note that this time the beads you will use to zip are the blues ones and the new beads are the yellow ones.

"I promise this isn't as complicated as it looks! The main thing to learn is what corners to add new beads into and what ones to share beads "

STEP 5
Continue joining pieces until you are ready to add your last one. This one only needs 2 new beads added - these sit in the centre front and back spots - all other beads are already there and shared.

STEP 6
You may want to then weave through all of the centre point beads on the front and back of your Star or Jack to join then ▯

> **TOP TIP**
> *If you find your Star or Jack is floppier than you'd like, stuff it with some wool, yarn or felt before fully joining your last piece*

Steps 3C

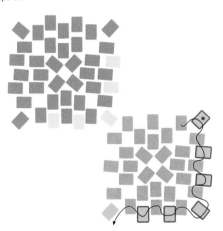

Steps 4

> **TOP TIP**
> *You need to make sure you fill in the last 2 sides of your square so that your next piece has the right beads to zip onto.*

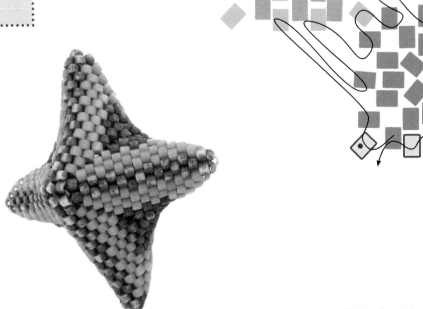

Jack Beaded Bead
Distorted Squares are perfect for beaded beads with added interest

Joining 3 or 4 Distorted Squares creates unique beaded beads that can be used in many different ways. How large, or small, you make them is entirely up to you; adding in patterns just gives you even more choice...

Materials
For each beaded bead
- 1–3g of size 11 cylinder beads

Colour advice
- Using 2 colours and alternating them every round gives you one type of stripe whereas changing after 2 rounds gives you a completely different one
- You could use a solid colour for a bold look or sprinkle in dots of another colour for a completely different effect

Sizing
Simply adding extra rounds of increasing makes for bigger Jacks

Using the beads
Jacks can be worn by threading a jump ring through one of the corner beads, joining them into lengths or hanging them like charms, or by threading through the hole created by the 4 beads at the start

Techniques
- Beading a Distorted Square, page 74
- Joining Distorted Squares, page 78

In a nutshell!
- Bead a Distorted Square then add a Point Round
- Bead another 2–3 Distorted Squares and zip them together

THE STEPS...

STEP 1
Following the basic instructions for beading a Distorted Square, make your first square as large as you choose, then add a Point Round.

STEP 2
Bead another Distorted Square the same size, but stop before you add the Point Round. Zip this to the first square and then add in the necessary beads for the next piece to zip to.

STEP 3
Bead a third, and if wanted, a fourth Distorted Square and zip these to the first two ⬚

Pay attention when zipping pieces together as where you add new beads makes all the difference

Sue Stallard's pastel Jack uses (from the middle out) DB1157, DB207, DB1505 and DB158

For this stunner Sue used DB7 and DB1013 to mix shiny and metallic

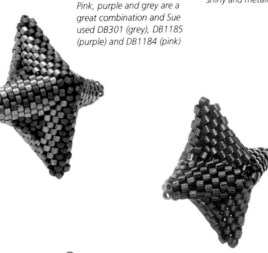

Pink, purple and grey are a great combination and Sue used DB301 (grey), DB1185 (purple) and DB1184 (pink)

For this bright orange Jack, Sue used DB603 (dark red), DB683 (lighter red), DB682 (dark orange) and DB681 (lighter orange)

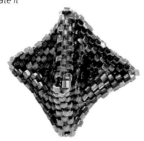

Brown and turquoise are always a winning combination and Sue used DB612 (brown) and DB918 (turquoise) to create it

For her blue and white variations Sue used DB200 for the white and then, in increasing order of dark to light: DB864, DB1578 and DB881

Star of Stars

Distorted Squares may look unexciting by themselves but when combined they can truly create wonderful things...

Beading Distorted Squares with a simple pattern leads to a star with a star pattern on it. This is the perfect chance to play around with colour and bead finish, as the basic pattern leaves you room to experiment and even just simple changes creates a whole new look. Adding a sixth Distorted Square as a bail creates a finished pendant

Materials
- 7g of size 11 cylinder for the background – your A beads
- 3g of size 11 cylinder beads in your highlight colour – your B beads

I used
- Copper – I used DB340
- Greens – a mix of any greens I liked the look of

Colour advice
You can use as few as 2 colours for this or as many as you desire if you want a mixed look
- Instead of a plain background why not mix up a great bead soup?
- Using the same colour, but in a matte and a metallic, would subtly show off the pattern

Sizing
Simply adding extra rounds of beadwork, even just in your background colour, at the end will create a larger star

Techniques
- Beading a Distorted Square, page 74
- Joining Distorted Squares, page 78

THE STEPS...
STEP 1
Following the Distorted Square beading instructions, and the pattern below, bead 5 Distorted Squares.

> **TOP TIP**
> * shows you where the beads you need to repeat to complete the round begin

Round 1 – A, B, A, B – thread through A to begin
Round 2 – A, A, A, A – squeeze these into the spaces between the beads added in Round 1
Round 3 – *2B, 2A
Round 4 – *2B, 1A, 2A, 1A
Round 5 – *2B, 1A, 1A, 2A, 1A, 1A
Round 6 – *2B, 1B, 1A, 1A, 2A, 1A, 1A, 1B
Round 7 – *2B, 1B, 1A, 1A, 1A, 2A, 1A, 1A, 1A, 1B
Round 8 – *2B, 1B, 1A, 1A, 1A, 1A, 2A, 1A, 1A, 1A, 1A, 1B
Round 9 – *2B, 1B, 1A, 1A, 1A, 1A, 1A, 2A, 1A, 1A, 1A, 1A, 1A, 1B
Round 10 – *2B, 1B, 1A, 1A, 1A, 1A, 1A, 1A, 2A, 1A, 1A, 1A, 1A, 1A, 1A, 1B
Round 11 – *2B, 1B, 1A, 1A, 1A, 1A, 1A, 1A, 1A, 2A, 1A, 1A, 1A, 1A, 1A, 1A, 1A, 1B
Round 12 – *2B, 1B, 1A, 1A, 1A, 1A, 1A, 1A, 1A, 1A, 2A, 1A, 1A, 1A, 1A, 1A, 1A, 1A, 1A, 1B

Round 13 – The Point Round – only needed initially for the first piece
*1B, 1B, 1B, 1A, 1A, 1A, 1A, 1A, 1A, 1A, 1A, 1A, 1A, 1A, 1A, 1A, 1A, 1A, 1A, 1B, 1B

STEP 2
Zip the pieces together with the pattern sitting at centre front and back.

If you want to add a bail:
STEP 3
Bead a Distorted Square using just your A beads until 10 along a side.

STEP 4
Add a Point Round to your bail but when you're beading 2 opposite corners, thread through a outside corner bead on your star to attach ☐

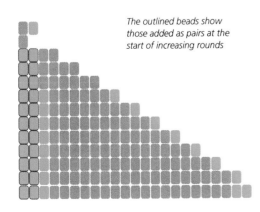

The outlined beads show those added as pairs at the start of increasing rounds

> *Pay attention to the pattern to get the pieces all the same*

The outlined beads show the first beads added at the start of each round

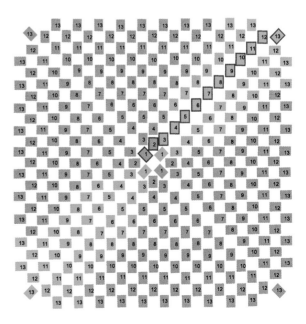

In a nutshell!

- Bead 5 Distorted Squares using the chart. Add a Point Round to only the first to begin with
- Zip the pieces together
- Bead a plain Distorted Square and add if you want a bail

Stripes are easy to bead in a star, and changing colour gives you a different look

Deborah Skelton's star uses DB878 (teal) and DB172, DB774, DB791 and DB727 (reds)

❝Stars are endlessly variable so experiment with the size, number of points, colours and patterns to create a night sky's worth!❞

How your Distorted Square will look before you begin joining them together

Playing around with the patterns you bead on your Distorted Squares has a dramatic effect on your finished star

"Go monochrome, but don't think that limits you to black and white. Monochrome can also mean varying shades of one colour so imagine this necklace in stripes of reds, blues, greens, oranges..."

Using simple stripes in black and white has a dramatic effect

Open Stars

Beaded stars are delights in themselves but the addition of hanging holes makes them so much more versatile

Integral hanging holes gives you much more variation with your Star. You can make the hanging method part of the star, as I have done with this project, or thread your finished star onto a chain or beaded rope

Materials
- 8g of size 11 cylinder beads
- 25mm Polaris ring (or other ring of your choice, you just may need to adjust your sizing)

I used
- Blue – DB756
- Copper – DB40

Techniques
- Herringbone Increase, page 19
- Distorted Square, page 74
- Joining Squares, page 78
- Triangle Openings, page 68

> **TOP TIP**
> *You will need to add a hole to two of your Distorted Squares if you just want to make one hanging hole*

In a nutshell!
- Increase a Distorted Square until 4 beads a side
- Skip adding beads in one corner for 5 rounds
- On the next round add in the missing beads, threading through your ring
- Bead 1 increasing round then a Point Round
- Repeat to make a second Distorted Square, zip to the first
- Bead your next 3 Distorted Square and zip as you would a regular Star

> **TOP TIP**
> *To calculate how many beads to pick up: it's 4 for each round where you added nothing in the corner, plus 2*

THE STEPS...

STEP 1
Begin beading a Distorted Square until you have 4 beads a side then add nothing in your first corner for 5 rounds. Always make sure you Step-Up at the end of the round to exit the first bead you added.

STEP 2
As you bead the next round, when you reach the end, pick up 22 beads and thread through your ring. Join the beads onto the beginning of the round again, making sure you Step-Up.

Step 1

STEP 3
Bead your next round of the Distorted Square as normal and when you reach the threaded-on beads peyote 5 single beads, bead a Herringbone Increase, then 5 single peyote stitches.

> **TOP TIP**
> *You bead a single peyote stitch for each round where you added nothing in the corner*

STEP 4
Bead your Point Round and then make one more Distorted Square using Steps 1-3, zipping it to the Point Round of the first square.

STEP 5
Bead 3 more squares and zip as you would a regular Star.

STEP 6
Bead a Distorted Square until 15 beads a side. When adding the Point Round, zip two opposite corners together to form a bail around the ring □

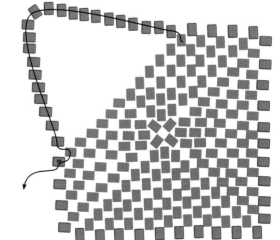

Step 2

Pentagons

Five sides, which demand
extra care and concentration
but reward you with exciting
possibilities...

Beading a Pentagon
A complicated thread path - but worth it!

Pentagons are 5-sided shapes and, like all the other shapes, they have a repeating series of steps to create them. However, unlike the Triangle you can't simply add increases on top of increases or your work will distort (see 'Distorted Square' on page 74 for another example of this)

Instead you will spread your increases out over a number of rounds so that the work increases at a more gradual rate. You will also use a clever little 'ladder stitch' increase which increases the number of beads you have in a round without squeezing any new ones in

Starting a basic pentagon

THE STEPS...
STEP 1
Your first round. Begin with 5 beads; join them into a circle by threading through the first bead. Don't tie these into a knot – give them room to move.

> **TOP TIP**
> *In these diagrams each round (and its repeated version) will be a different colour so you can keep track of where the beads sit*

STEP 2
Round 2 - Add 1 bead between each of those in the previous round (in future repeats this includes 1 either side of the 'stitched-on' bead).

STEP 3
Round 3 - Using a Herringbone Increase, add 2 beads into each space; this forms the corners (in future repeats you will also have side spaces which require just 1 bead)

STEP 4
Round 4 - Peyote stitch 1 bead in every space, including splitting the 2 corner beads.

STEP 5
Now for the fun part! This is an unusual increase but a simple one. Ladder stitch (or square stitch if you prefer to think of it that way) 1 bead onto every corner bead and then peyote stitch one bead into every side space.

It is very important that at the end of your round you don't try to Step-Up into the added-on corner bead. Always Step-Up so you exit the first side bead you added.

STEP 6
Continuing a pentagon increase You now need to simply repeat Steps 2-5 until your pentagon is the size you require. As you do this the number of side spaces you have will increase but you always just put 1 bead into these (unless you're trying something fancy, that is…)

The diagram shows a pentagon with one more repeat of Steps 2 - 5 so you can see that all of the increasing just occurs at the corners

Step 1

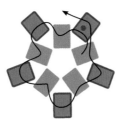
Step 2

Step 3

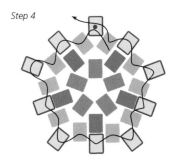
Step 4

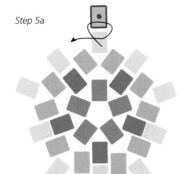
Step 5a

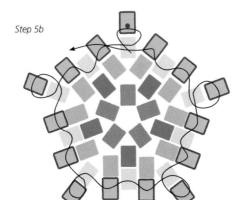
Step 5b

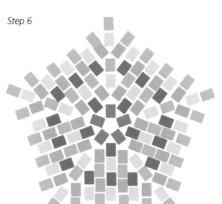
Step 6

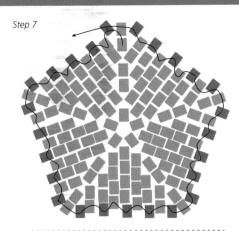

Step 7

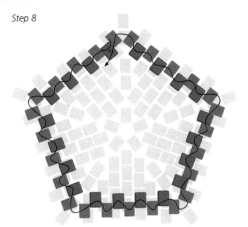

Step 8

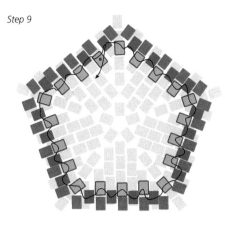

Step 9

> **Point Round**
> Any time you want to stop increasing, you can do use any of the rounds where you add a single bead into each space, including the corners (e.g. rounds 2, 4 or 5) as a Point Round

Decreasing a pentagon

There is a set pattern for decreasing a pentagon due to its more complicated thread path. Just as with increasing we don't want to decrease every round otherwise your work will distort

Please note that it is very important you follow the directions for Steps 9 and 10 correctly otherwise you'll end up adding extra beads and your work will never decrease!

Just as with all decreasing you need to begin by adding a round where you put a single bead either side of your corner spaces

From now on the diagrams will show all of your increasing rounds the same colour (and then greyed out) and just the decreasing rounds will change

STEP 7
Peyote 1 bead in every space (including each side of any 'stitched-on' beads in repeats if appropriate).

STEP 8
Peyote 1 bead in every space, except for the corners. Here you will bead a Peyote Decrease by threading through your work as through you are beading peyote stitch but not adding a bead.

The beads in your previous round will pull into the centre - but this can take a few rounds until it sits comfortably.

STEP 9
Peyote 1 bead in every space, including 1 in every corner. Make sure you pull this round tight so the work begins to decrease. If you don't do this it can cause problems in the next round.

STEP 10

Before stitching this round, check the diagrams to ensure you don't make a mistake - it's very easy to, especially if you are only adding 5 beads in your round (when you have decreased right down). The urge is to try and sneak more in! - resist the urge!

Stitch 1 bead to each corner bead and add 1 bead in each side space if appropriate, but NOT in the side spaces which sit either side of the bead added into the corners in the previous round - there aren't really any spaces there, it can just look as though there are if your work hasn't pulled in tight yet.

Step-Up at the end of the round to be exiting one of your side beads, NOT one of the new stitched-on corner beads.

On this second diagram everywhere there is a star is where you don't want to accidentally add a bead

STEP 11
Continuing a pentagon decrease
You're now back at the equivalent of Step 7. Repeat Steps 7-10 until it is the size you require. This diagram shows a pentagon decreased right down to just 5 beads in the last round.

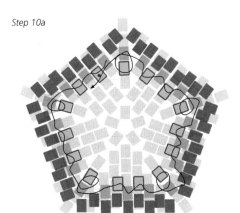

Step 10a

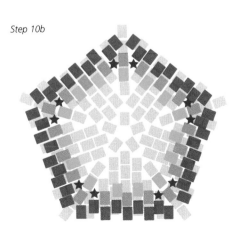

Step 10b

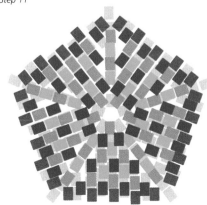

Step 11

Pentagon Star Beaded Bead

Take a pentagon and add a larger hole... instant geometric delights

Playing around with pentagons with larger holes in the centre can lead to many different ideas and uses. As long as you remember they're easier than you think they are, you should be OK!

Materials
For one small beaded bead
- 1g of size 11 cylinder beads – your A beads
- 1g of size 11 cylinder beads – your B beads

I used
- Matte Copper – DB340
- Blue – DB165

Colour and pattern
There are so many ways you could vary these. Add in stripes, dots and other shapes for patterns. Play with bead finishes to alter the look without having to do anything complicated

Size and shape
Increase more for bigger pentagons. Pick up more beads at the start for larger holes

Using them
The pentagons can be used as beaded beads. They can be hung from one of the corner beads using a jump ring or they can be made interlinked to create a chain. You're only limited by your imagination…

Techniques
- Beading a Pentagon, page 90

THE STEPS...
Getting started
STEP 1
Pick up 10A beads and circle through the first two to join into a circle. Add a single round of circular peyote stitch using A beads for a total of 3 rounds.

> **TOP TIP**
> *Circling through 2 beads means your tail is in the right place to use when you return to it at Step 9*

Step 1

Step 2

> **TOP TIP**
> *Keep an eye on your Step-Up. Remember that when increasing a pentagon there is one place your Step-Up will vary*

In a nutshell!
- Using a number of beads that's a multiple of 10, bead an odd number of rounds of circular peyote
- Bead a pentagon until it's the size you want and then bead a Point Round
- Return to the start of your work and replicate the increase, ensuring the corners line up
- Zip the edges together

Increasing the first side
STEP 2
Bead using Herringbone Increases to add 2A into every space. This adds your corner spaces.

STEP 3
*Use a Herringbone Increase to add 2A beads into the first space, then peyote 1B bead into second. Repeat from * all the way around the circle.

Step 3

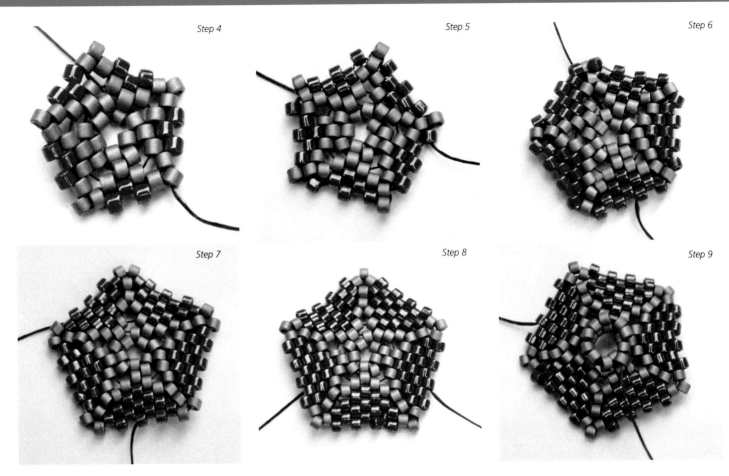

Step 4 *Step 5* *Step 6*

Step 7 *Step 8* *Step 9*

STEP 4
Peyote 1 bead in every space, including splitting the 2 corner beads, in the order A, B, B. Repeat to the end.

STEP 5
Add 1B bead into every side space, and ladder stitch 1A to each corner bead. At the end you need to Step-Up to be exiting one of your side beads.

STEP 6
Add 1B bead into every space, including either side of the 'stitched on' bead from Step 5.

STEP 7
Add 1B bead into every side space and 2A into each corner.

Point Round
STEP 8
Peyote 1 bead into every space, including splitting the corner pairs, in the order B, B, A, B, B – repeat.

The other side
STEP 9
Return to the thread you left at the start. You can now decide whether you want to increase the depth at the centre of your work. If you do decide to do this you need to add an even number of extra rounds so your corners line up. I decided to add 2 more rounds using 1A in every space.

STEP 10
Bead Steps 2–7 as you did for the first side.

STEP 11
Zip together your last round on the second side by going through all the beads added in the Point Round on the first side. This will bring the two sides together into a solid piece □

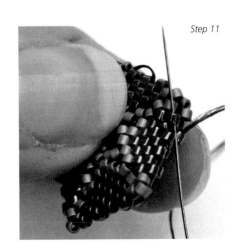

Step 11

Pentagon Bangle
Combine a 5-sided pentagon with a 4-sided diamond for a simple but effective motif

This bangle uses large shapes and more rounds of plain beading to work up quicker (less increasing and decreasing saves time!) with a plain motif, which can be played around with in many ways. This basic design also works well as simple beaded beads for a different look

Materials
- 22g of size 11 cylinder beads in a mix of blues – your A beads
- 8g of size 11 cylinder beads in matte black – your B beads
- 4g of size 11 cylinder beads in bronze – your C beads

I used
- Blues – a mix of DB730, DB756, DB920, DB377 and DB165
- Black – DB310
- Bronze – DB22

Variations – Colours
Why not have your B and C beads the same? This would give you a solid diamond on each side of your bangle. You could also have your A and C beads the same so your diamond pattern is just a simple outline. You could even just do the whole bangle in one colour, or a random mix, for a solid look with no pattern

Sizing
This piece is easy to size, as you create its length as you go. But be aware than it's quite firm and as there is no plain peyote between increases and decreases your work won't be as flexible as if there were

Techniques
- Beading a Pentagon, page 90
- Zipping and Joining, page 22

THE STEPS...

STEP 1
Increasing section – Pick up 5A beads and circle through the first one to join into a circle.

STEP 2
Using circular peyote stitch, add 1A into every space between each bead added in Step 1.

STEP 3
Herringbone Increase, adding 2A in every space.

STEP 4
Peyote 1A in every space, including splitting the pairs added in Step 3.

STEP 5
*Ladder stitch on 1A; peyote 1A into each of the next two spaces. Repeat from * four times more to finish the round. Step-Up at the end of the round to exit the first 'side bead' added.

STEP 6
Peyote 1A bead into every space, including either side of the 'stitched-on' beads.

STEP 7
*Peyote 1A, 2A, 1A into the next three spaces. Repeat from * four times more to finish the round.

STEP 8
Point Round – Add 1A in every space, including splitting the pairs added in Step 7.

STEP 9
Peyote 1A bead into every space.

STEP 10
*Peyote 1A, 1A, 1B, 1A. Repeat from * four times more to finish the round.

STEP 11
*Peyote 1A, 1B, 1B, 1A. Repeat from * four times more to finish the round.

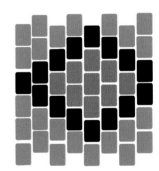

This chart shows you the beads you will use on each side of your pentagon for Steps 9–20. Note that the column on the left hand-side shows the beads that will sit in the corner spaces and the chart will repeat for each side

In a nutshell!
- Increase a pentagon until you have 4 beads along a side then add a Point Round
- Bead pentagon sides using the chart for the pattern
- Decrease your pentagon until 1 bead per side
- Increase again and continue adding pentagon sections until your bangle is as long as you need
- Remove starter rounds and zip ends together

TOP TIP
Keep an eye on your Step-Up. There are some points (Steps 5, 23, 24, 26) where you need to Step-Up into the correct bead for the design to work

STEP 12

*Peyote 1B, 1C, 1B, 1A. Repeat from * four times more to finish the round.

STEP 13

*Peyote 1C, 1C, 1B, 1B. Repeat from * four times more to finish the round.

STEP 14

*Peyote 1C, 1C, 1B, 1C. Repeat from * four times more to finish the round.

STEP 15

*Peyote 1C, 1B, 1B, 1C. Repeat from * four times more to finish the round.

STEP 16

*Peyote 1B, 1A, 1B, 1C. Repeat from * four times more to finish the round.

STEP 17

*Peyote 1A, 1A, 1B, 1B. Repeat from * four times more to finish the round.

STEP 18

*Peyote 1A, 1A, 1B, 1A. Repeat from * four times more to finish the round.

STEP 19

Peyote 1A bead into every space.

STEP 20

Peyote 1A bead into every space.

STEP 21

Peyote 1A bead into every space.

STEP 22

You'll now begin to decrease, so ensure you pull your work nice and tight. *Peyote 1A, 1A, add nothing in the next space (a peyote decrease), 1A. Repeat from * four times more to finish the round.

STEP 23

Add 1A bead into every space, including the large space at each corner. Finish the round by ensuring you Step-Up to a corner bead.

STEP 24

*Ladder stitch on 1A, peyote 1A into the single side space. Repeat from * four times more to finish the round. Step-Up at the end of the round to exit the first 'side bead' added.

STEP 25

Add 1A bead into every space.

STEP 26

*Add nothing into the corner space (a peyote decrease), 1A into the side space. Repeat from * four times more to finish the round. Step-Up at the end of the round to exit the first 'side bead' added.

STEP 27

You are now back at the equivalent of Step 3. Continue peyote stitching with patterns of increasing and decreasing until your bangle is as long as you desire.

STEP 28

You are now ready to zip the ends together. This will be easier to do if you undo the rounds added in Steps 1–7
(you will know you have removed enough when you have a round with one bead in each corner rather than two). Then bead the end of your work up to Step 7 and use the beads at the start to replicate adding Step 8 □

TOP TIP

On Step 24 make sure you don't try to add in any extra beads, or your work won't decrease

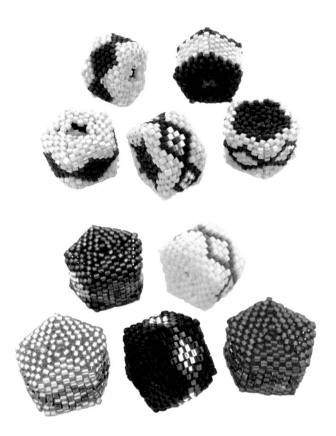

Beading Steps 1–26 will give you a simple beaded bead, as Jo Prowse, Candys S. McCulley, Cate Jones and Tina Holmes did with these

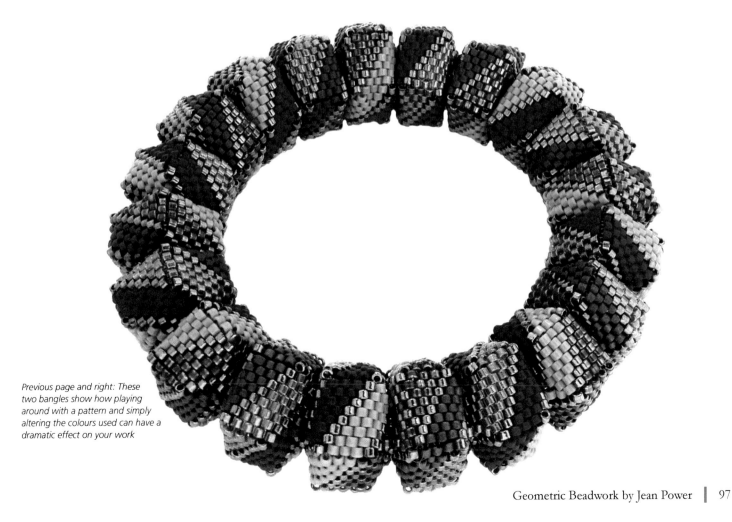

Previous page and right: These two bangles show how playing around with a pattern and simply altering the colours used can have a dramatic effect on your work

Pentagon Secret
Use pentagons to create a pendant with a hidden secret...

The basic principles of pentagon increasing and decreasing are put to use here to create a 2-in-1 project: a pendant that is also a vessel. All it takes is some increasing and decreasing to shape and mould a piece that grows just as much or as little as you want it to. Adding your method of hanging as you work means that by the time you're finished beading it's all done and ready to wear

You might think that adding jump rings is a pain as they get in your way as you bead, but it's much easier than trying to attach a chain later on!

Materials and tools
- 5g of size 11 cylinder beads in your edging colour – your A beads
- 6g of size 11 cylinder beads in your highlight colour – your B beads
- 1 fine chain
- A small number of jump rings that will easily thread through a cylinder bead
- 2 pairs of flat pliers to open and close your jump rings

I used
- Bronze - I used DB22
- Mix – I used 25 different tubes of beads with a few as a single bead left in them to create my mix

Colour advice
You don't have to use two different colours for this project – the same colour but with different bead finishes would give a subtle but effective look

Techniques used
- Beading a Pentagon, page 90

Sizing
- Exactly the same piece but beaded in size 15 cylinder beads would be smaller and more subtle. You may find that the bead you add your jump ring to will still need to be a size 11 cylinder
- Following the same steps, but in size 10 cylinders, will give a bigger, bolder pendant

THE STEPS...
The body of the pendant
STEP 1
Pick up 5A beads and circle through the first one to join into a circle.

STEP 2
Peyote stitch using 1A bead in between all the 5 beads.

STEP 3
Ladder stitch a single bead to any one of the beginning 5 beads and thread a jump ring through it. As your beadwork grows, add extra jump rings to make a small chain until you are told to add your actual chain.

From now on you will use basic circular peyote stitch and increasing and decreasing a pentagon, using the beads described to create the pattern

STEP 4
Use a Herringbone Increase to add 2A into every space.

STEP 5
Peyote stitch 1A into every space, including splitting the pairs added in the previous round.

STEP 6
Peyote stitch 1A into every space.

STEP 7
*Peyote 1A, 2A. Repeat from * to complete the round.

STEP 8
Peyote stitch 1A into every space, including splitting the pairs added in the previous round.

STEP 9
*Peyote 1A, ladder stitch on 1A, peyote stitch 1A, 1A. Repeat from * to complete the round.

STEP 10
Peyote stitch 1B into every space, including either side of the 'stitched-on' beads in the previous round.

STEP 11
You will now stop increasing for a few rounds, so pull your work tight to ensure it pulls in nicely.
*Peyote 1A, 1B, 1B, 1B. Repeat from * to complete the round. Step-Up to exit the first new B added – this is essential.

STEP 12
Peyote stitch 1B into every space.

STEP 13
*Peyote 1B, 1B, 1A, 1B. Repeat from * to finish the round.

Pay attention to your Step-Up because, as with all pentagon beading, you sometimes need to alter the bead you go through

In a nutshell!
- Bead a series of pentagon increases with rounds of plain beadwork to add height, making sure to enclose your chain as you go
- Decrease to bead the lip of the vessel
- Bead a pentagon lid to match

STEP 14
Peyote stitch 1B into every space.

STEP 15
Peyote stitch 1A into every space.

STEP 16
Peyote stitch 1A into every space.

STEP 17
You're now going to increase again. *Peyote 2A, 1A, 1A, 1A. Repeat from * to finish the round.

STEP 18
Peyote stitch 1A into every space, including splitting the pairs added in the previous round.

STEP 19
*Peyote 1A, 1A, 1A, 1A, 1A, ladder stitch on 1A. Repeat from * to finish the round, ensuring you Step-Up to exit the first 1A added.

STEP 20
Peyote stitch 1A into every space, including either side of the 'stitched-on' beads in the previous round.

STEP 21
You will now stop increasing for a few rounds, so pull your work tight to ensure it pulls in nicely. *Peyote 1B, 1B, 1B, 1B, 1A, 1B. Repeat from * to finish the round.

STEP 22
Peyote stitch 1B into every space.

STEP 23
*Peyote 1B, 1B, 1B, 1A, 1B, 1B. Repeat from * to finish the round.

STEP 24
Peyote stitch 1B into every space.

STEP 25
*Peyote 1B, 1B, 1A, 1B, 1B, 1B. Repeat from * to finish the round.

STEP 26
Peyote stitch 1B into every space.

STEP 27
*Peyote 1B, 1A, 1B, 1B, 1B, 1B. Repeat from * to finish the round.

STEP 28
Peyote stitch 1A into every space.

STEP 29. You're now going to increase again. *Herringbone Increase 2A then peyote 1A, 1A, 1A, 1A, 1A. Repeat from * to finish the round.

STEP 30
Peyote stitch 1A into every space, including splitting the pairs added in the previous round.

STEP 31
*Peyote 1A, 1A, 1A, 1A, 1A, 1A, 1A, ladder stitch on 1A. Repeat from * to finish the round, ensuring you Step-Up to exit the first 1A added.

STEP 32
Peyote stitch 1A into every space, including either side of the 'stitched-on' beads in the previous round.

STEP 33
You will now stop increasing for a few rounds so pull your work tight *Peyote 1B, 1B, 1B, 1B, 1B, 1B, 1A, 1B. Repeat from * to finish the round.

STEP 34
Peyote stitch 1B into every space.

STEP 35
*Peyote 1B, 1B, 1B, 1B, 1B, 1A, 1B, 1B. Repeat from * to finish the round.

STEP 36
Peyote stitch 1B into every space.

STEP 37
*Peyote 1B, 1B, 1B, 1B, 1A, 1B, 1B, 1B. Repeat from * to finish the round.

STEP 38
Peyote stitch 1B into every space.

> **TOP TIP**
> You'll soon need to add both ends of your chain to the jump ring chain so that the vessel can be a pendant. Add this whenever you feel you can, remembering not to try to add it too late!

STEP 39
*Peyote 1B, 1B, 1B, 1A, 1B, 1B, 1B, 1B. Repeat from * to finish the round.

STEP 40
Peyote stitch 1B into every space.

STEP 41
*Peyote 1B, 1B, 1A, 1B, 1B, 1B, 1B, 1B. Repeat from * to finish the round.

STEP 42. Peyote stitch 1A into every space.

STEP 43. You're now going to decrease, so make sure you pull your work nice and tight * Peyote 1A, nothing in the next space, 1A, 1A, 1A, 1A, 1A, 1A. Repeat from * to finish the round. Step-Up to exit the first A bead added this round.

STEP 44
Peyote stitch 1A into every space, including the corner where you added nothing in the last round.

Left and right: Altering the pattern you bead as you go, as well as the amount you increase or don't increase, can lead to all sorts of variations

STEP 45
You are now going to decrease, so you must ensure that you don't add too many beads in the next round. Remember back to your Pentagon decreasing and look out for those spaces where you won't add any beads. *Ladder stitch on 1A then peyote 1A, 1A, 1A, 1A, 1A. Repeat from * to finish the round, ensuring you Step-Up to exit the second 1A added.

STEP 46
Peyote 1A in every space, including either side of the 'stitched-on' bead from Step 45.

STEP 47
*Peyote 1A, 1A, 1A, 1A then nothing in the next space, then 1A. Repeat from * to finish the round.

STEP 48
You'll now stop decreasing and bead the 'lip' of your vessel. Peyote stitch 1A into every space, including the corner where you added nothing in the last round.

STEP 49
Peyote stitch 1A into every space.

STEP 50
Peyote stitch 1A into every space.

STEP 51
Peyote stitch 1A into every space.

STEP 52
Peyote stitch 1A into every space.

The lid
This is beaded in a similar way to the pendant

STEP 1
Pick up 15A and join into a circle by threading through the first bead.

STEP 2
*Squeeze in 1A into the gap between the next 2 beads and then peyote stitch 1A into the next space. Repeat from * to add a total of 10A beads and complete the round.

STEP 3
Peyote stitch 1A into every space.

STEP 4
Bead Steps 7–27 of the body to complete your lid. Thread onto your chain ▯

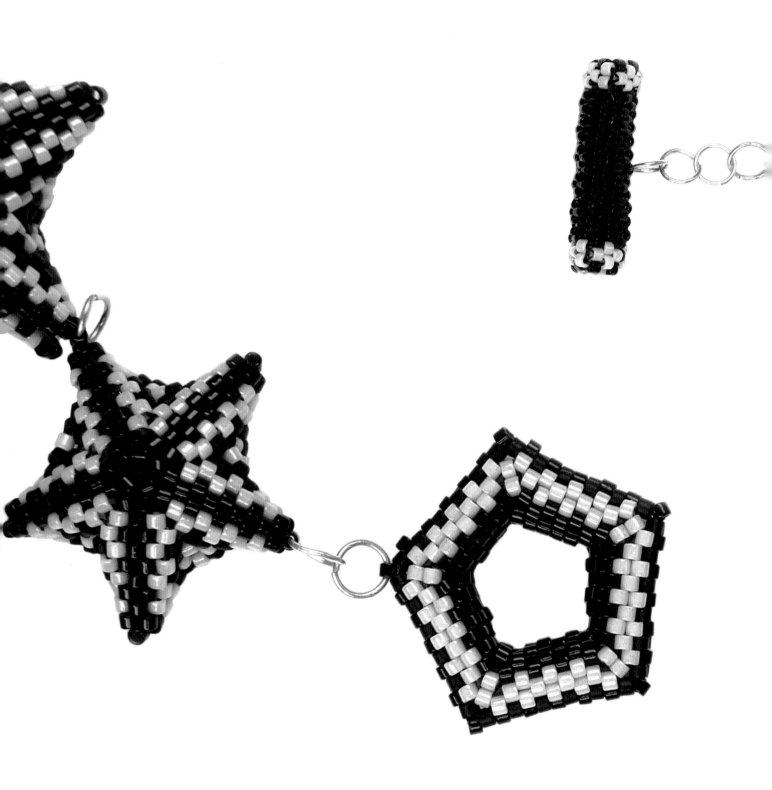

Pentagon Clasp
A pentagon clasp is ideal for finishing your beadwork

Beading a pentagon with a larger centre hole means it can be used as the loop on a clasp, a link in a chain, a beaded bead, the end of a lariat...

Materials
- 1g of size 11 cylinder beads in black – your A beads
- 1g of Size 11 cylinder beads in cream – your B beads

I used
- Black- DB10
- Cream- DB203

Sizing
These links are easy to size – you simply begin with a number of beads which is a multiple of 10

Techniques used
- Beading a Pentagon, page 90
- Zipping and Joining, page 22

THE STEPS...
STEP 1
Pick up 30A beads and join into a circle by threading through the first 6.

STEP 2
Using circular peyote stitch, add one round using A beads.

STEP 3
*Herringbone Increase adding 2A in first space then peyote stitch 1A into the next 2 spaces. Repeat from * to complete the round.

STEP 4
Peyote 1B in every space, including splitting the pairs added in step 3.

STEP 5
*Ladder stitch on 1B, peyote 1B into each of the next four spaces. Repeat from * four times more to finish the round. Step-Up at the end of the round to exit the first 'side bead' added.

STEP 6
Peyote 1B bead into every space, including either side of the 'stitched on' beads.

STEP 7
*Peyote 1A, 1A, 1A, Herringbone Increase using 2A, peyote stitch 1A. Repeat from * four times more to finish the round.

STEP 8
Point Round – Add 1A in every space, including splitting the pairs added in Step 7. Weave away this thread.

STEP 9
Return to your tail thread and repeat Steps 3–8 on the second side.

STEP 10
Zip the edges of your beadwork together □

Gemma Ingram beaded a pentagon that started with a circle of 30 beads, and linked them together every time she picked up her next line of 30. She beaded 10 using DB47, DB63, DB167, DB178, DB243, DB659, DB755, DB756, DB920 and DB1597

TOP TIP
This will mean your tail thread is in the right place for you to carry on at Step 9 without having to weave through your work

In a nutshell!
- Pick up a multiple of 10 beads and bead circular peyote as much as desired
- Increase to a pentagon, then bead a Point Round
- Return to your tail thread and increase the second side of your work
- Zip edges together

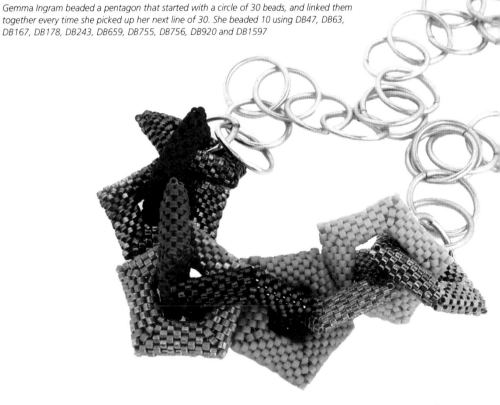

Beyond Corners

It's time to stop thinking in terms
of corners but instead embrace
horns, rick-racks
and a whole lot more...

Horned Bangle

This bangle is an ideal introduction to the world of increasing, decreasing, geometric shaping... and of course horns!

A lot easier to bead than it looks, this bangle takes the simple process of increasing and decreasing you do for all other geometric work and turns it on its head to create a spiked cuff that can be as fearsome or as subtle as you choose.

Materials
- 9g size 11 cylinder beads in your horn colour
- 9g size 11 cylinder beads in your bangle colour

Techniques
- Herringbone Increase, page 19
- Peyote Decrease, page 21

I used
- Copper – DB40
- Blues – An even mix of DB47, DB285 and DB707

Sizing and horn placement
You want to begin by picking up an even number of beads that will easily slide over your hand onto your wrist. Your beading will slightly decrease the size as you go, so take this into account.

You want your horns evenly spaced approximately every 20 beads (10 gaps): I made 9 horns and began with 180 beads. I would begin by finding a number of beads that fits you and calculate the number of horns and their placement from this.

Some examples are:
- 144 beads – 8 horns with 1 every 18 beads (9 gaps)
- 160 beads – 8 horns with 1 every 20 beads (10 gaps)
- 162 beads – 9 horns with 1 every 18 beads (9 gaps)
- 180 beads – 9 horns with 1 every 20 beads (10 gaps)
- 200 beads – 10 horns with 1 every 20 beads (10 gaps)

In a nutshell!
- Beginning with bangle beads
  - Calculate size and pick this number of beads up for first 2 rounds
  - Bead tubular peyote for 2 rounds
- Begin to sprinkle in your horn beads, increasing their use up to the Point Round and then decreasing their quantity as you bead the other side
  - Beads 7 rounds with Herringbone Increases spaced evenly around
  - Bead the Point Round then one round of peyote stitch
  - Bead 7 rounds with Peyote Decreases in the same spots as your increases
  - Bead 3 rounds of tubular peyote
- *Switch to horn beads
  - Bead 1 round of peyote stitch
  - Bead 1 round with a decrease in all of the spots you previously decreased
  - 1 round of peyote with a bead in every space
- Return to your tail thread and repeat from * to finish

TOP TIP
If you want to decrease your finished piece some more then continue adding rounds of decreasing beadwork along each edge

TOP TIP
Don't panic! This project won't look as though it will horn until you've done the decreasing. You can help it by making sure it's twisting the right way, etc., but bear with it and be patient

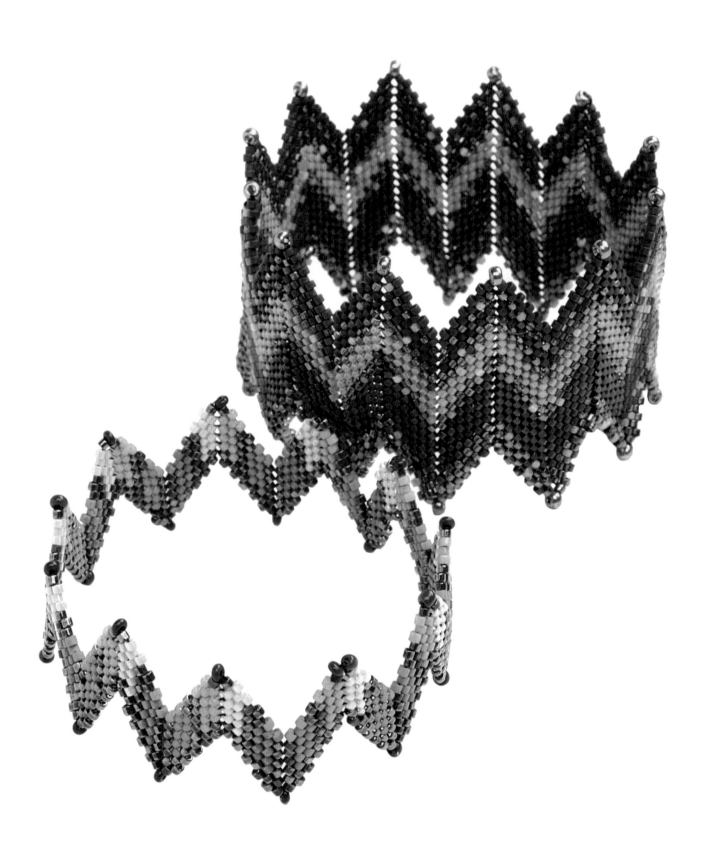

Rick-Rack Bangle

Turn increasing and decreasing on its head with this bangle that magically develops angles as you go

Bear with it! It can take a good few rounds for the work to sit as it will when finished

Simple increases and decreases in peyote stitch do all sorts of wondrous things and this bangle is the perfect example of that. Although at first it may seem as though you're working with a ridiculous number of beads and not getting anywhere, stick with it; after a few rounds it all begins to make sense and soon a Rick-Rack beauty will be unveiling itself

Materials
- 15g of size 11 cylinder beads
- Small number of drop beads – see 'Sizing' for details. These are your 'point beads'

Variations
Colours – why not change bead colour every round? Keep the same colour throughout? Have each 'section' a different colour? For more help then check out 'Colour and Design' on page 14

You don't need to use drop beads; why not try a larger, or smaller, seed bead?

Sizing
When fully beaded this bangle shrinks by approximately 40% from the number of beads you first picked up. You can be exact and measure the size or guesstimate and see what happens – the choice is yours. In the bangle described here each section (which uses 2 drop beads) makes a finished size of 2cm or 6/8 of an inch. So for my finished piece of 24cm/ 9 inches I used 24 drop beads and picked up 12 repeats in Step 1.

Below are some approximate measurements from repeats – but beware, as every bead and colour of bead varies slightly in size there may be up to 1cm/ ½ inch difference in your finished piece.
- 6 repeats would give me a bangle measuring 12cm/ 4 ¾ inches and use 12 drop beads
- 7 repeats would give me a bangle measuring 14cm/ 5 ½ inches and use 14 drop beads
- 8 repeats would give me a bangle measuring 16cm/ 6 ¼ inches and use 16 drop beads
- 9 repeats would give me a bangle measuring 18cm/ 7 inches and use 18 drop beads
- 10 repeats would give me a bangle measuring 20cm/ 7 1/8 inches and use 20 drop beads
- 11 repeats would give me a bangle measuring 22cm/ 8 ¾ inches and use 22 drop beads

- 12 repeats would give me a bangle measuring 24cm/ 9 ½ inches and use 24 drop beads
- 13 repeats would give me a bangle measuring 26cm/ 10 ¼ inches and use 26 drop beads
- 14 repeats would give me a bangle measuring 28cm/ 11 inches and use 28 drop beads
- 15 repeats would give me a bangle measuring 30cm/ 11 ¾ inches and use 30 drop beads
- 16 repeats would give me a bangle measuring 32cm/ 12 ½ inches and use 32 drop beads
- 17 repeats would give me a bangle measuring 34cm/ ½ inches and use 34 drop beads

Techniques
- Herringbone Increase, page 19
- Peyote Decrease, page 21

In a nutshell!
- Work out the number of beads you need and pick up that amount
- Bead circular peyote stitch adding increases and decreases as you go
- Finish with a Point Round

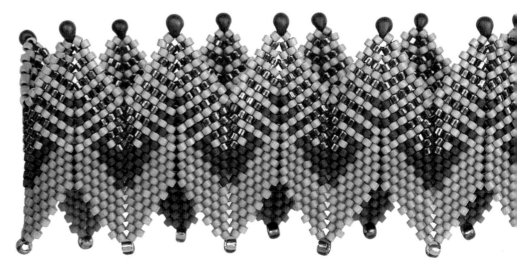

For this Rick-Rack I played with colour and stripes

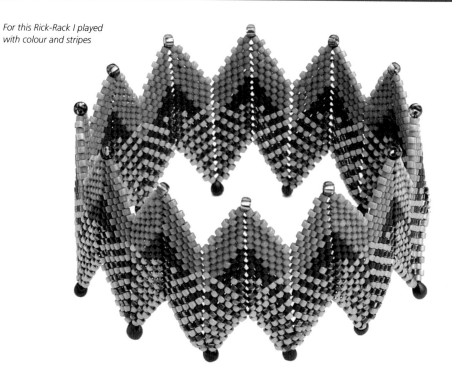

Below: This Rick-Rack beaded by Gabriella van Diepen (and wonderfully photographed by Jeroen Medema) shows just some of the amazing variations possible

Step 1

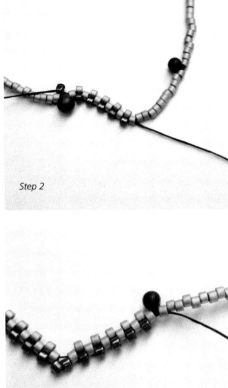

Step 2

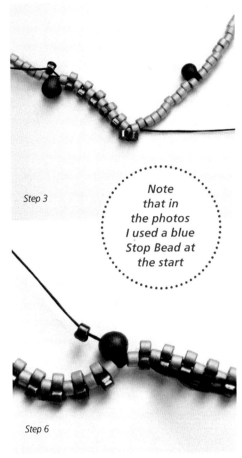

Step 3

Note that in the photos I used a blue Stop Bead at the start

Step 4

Step 5

Step 6

THE STEPS...
Increasing section
STEP 1
Pick up 22 cylinder beads and 1 drop bead. Repeat this pattern until you have picked up a strand of beads that is 40% longer than you want your finished piece to be. Thread through your first bead to join into a circle.

STEP 2
Using peyote stitch, add 1 cylinder bead into each of the next 5 spaces.

STEP 3
Add a Herringbone Increase into the next gap by squeezing 2 cylinder beads between the next two beads in your original strand. Make sure you don't get this mixed up with a peyote stitch and 'miss a bead' on your original strand; you must place it between two beads.

STEP 4
Using peyote stitch, add 1 cylinder bead into each of the next 5 spaces.

STEP 5
Add no beads into the next space but instead bead a Peyote Decrease. If your counting was right then this will be where your drop bead is. If it's not then check your beading, especially how you did your Herringbone Increase in Step 3.

STEP 6
Repeat Steps 2–4 all the way around your original strand. At the end of the round, ensure you Step-Up to exit the first bead added in this round.

STEP 7
Continue adding rounds of beadwork in exactly the same way but changing colour whenever you desire until you have added a total of 21 rounds. You can of course add fewer if you wish, but you will find it takes at least 6–8 rounds before the size has shrunk right down.

STEP 8
Bead your last round in the same manner but replacing your 2 beads added into an increase with 1 drop bead □

Step 7

TOP TIP
I always recommend that after you have beaded the third round you stop and check your work. You need to ensure that all your increases and decreases are going the same way and that your work hasn't twisted. If it has gone wrong you have 2 options: 1– start again... 2 – give your work a big twist where it's wrong and literally make the points go in the same direction. This may seem odd at first but as you carry on beading it will all fall into shape and I often end up doing this... don't tell anyone!

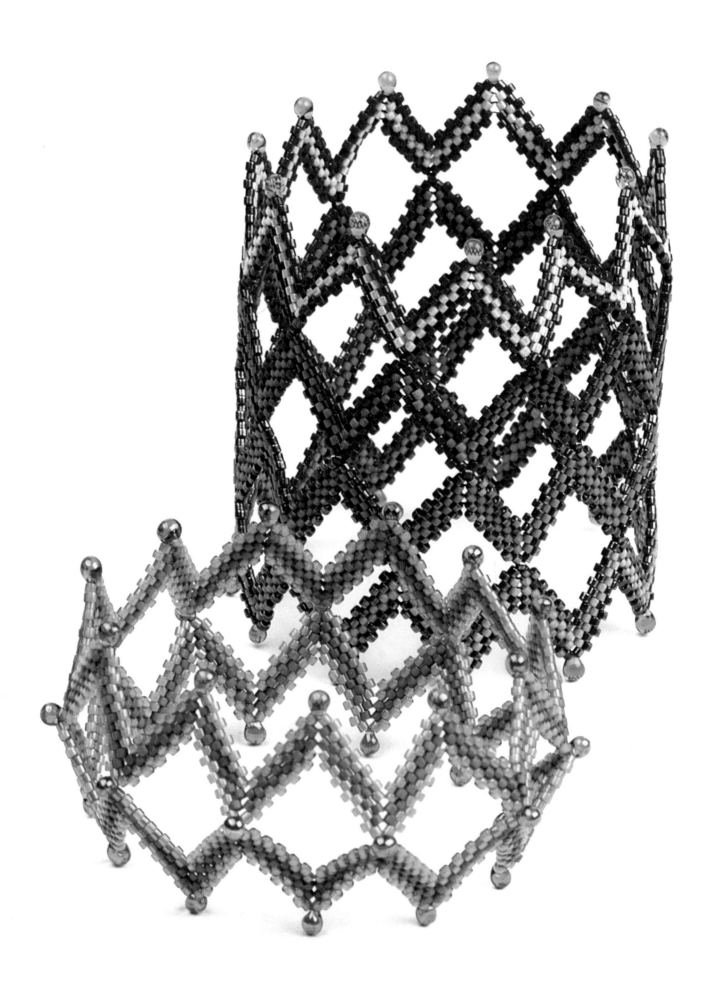

Double Rick-Rack

The obvious next step after one Rick-Rack is two Rick-Racks...

Materials
- 10g of size 11 cylinder beads
- Small number of feature beads – see 'Sizing' on Rick-Rack Bangle, page 108

Techniques
- Herringbone Increase, page 19
- Peyote Decrease, page 21
- Rick-Rack Bangle, page 108

> **TOP TIP**
> *I really recommend beading a basic Rick-Rack before you begin so that you are familiar with the ideas*

I used
- Dark blue – DB165
- Cream – DB205
- Brown – DB653
- Matte blue – DB798
- Pink – DB1363
- Brown - DB653
- Green - DB272

Starting doubled

Doubling up
There are two ways you can bead a double Rick-Rack: beginning the second right off the first or joining them together at the end – the choice is yours.

Starting doubled
Once you've beaded one Rick-Rack as high as you want it, weave through to exit one of the 'point beads' on the last round. Pick up the same number of cylinder beads as you did for each section when you beaded your first Rick-Rack and then thread through the next 'point bead' on the first Rick-Rack. Repeat this all the way around, making sure you Step-Up at the end to exit the first cylinder bead picked up. Then bead your Rick-Rack as before…

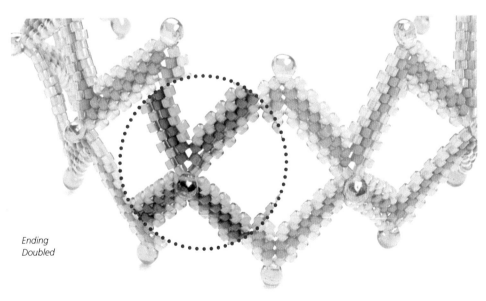

Ending Doubled

Ending Doubled
Bead your first and second Rick-Racks separately, but when you wish to add your last round on the second one instead of picking up a new 'point bead', thread through ones on your first Rick-Rack, zipping them together ⬜

In a nutshell!
- Bead a Rick-Rack
- Attach another Rick-Rack either before you begin, or as you end

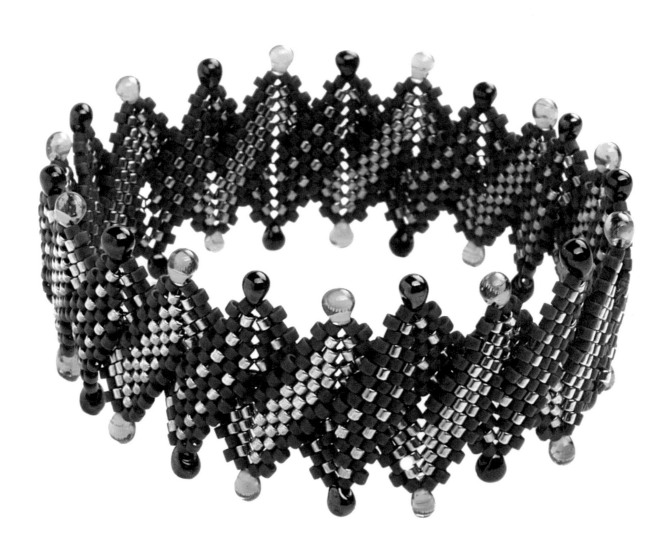

Layered Rick-Rack

The next step for Rick-Racks is layering them...

Materials
- 15g of size 11 cylinder beads
- Small number of feature beads – see 'Sizing' on Rick-Rack Bangle, page 108

Techniques
- Herringbone Increase, page 19
- Peyote Decrease, page 21
- Rick-Rack Bangle, page 108

> **TOP TIP**
> *I recommend beading a basic Rick-Rack before you begin so that you are familiar with the ideas*

I used
- Blue – DB750
- Pewter – DB21

Layering
Bead one Rick-Rack bangle as desired; mine is just 8 rounds high.

Pick up all the beads you need to begin another Rick-Rack, but before joining them into a circle, weave the length of beads under and over the 'V's of your first bangle.

The length will be far too long for this to be comfortable at first, but bear with it and make sure you don't make any mistakes when weaving.

Once woven, join the ends and bead the second Rick-Rack as usual; you will find that after a couple of rounds the work will settle into place and you can carry on □

> **TOP TIP**
> *I find that as I work my second Rick-Rack I am constantly rotating my work inside and out so I can see where I am and not have to work inside the other bangle*

In a nutshell!
- Bead a Rick-Rack
- Bead another Rick-Rack interlinked through the first

In a nutshell!

- Pick up the beads you need; see 'Sizing' and 'Getting started' for details
- Bead a flat Rick-Rack
- Attach to your clasp

Flat Rick-Rack

Perfect if you don't like bangles

Materials
- 10g of size 11 cylinder beads – your A beads
- A small number of feature beads for the points – your B beads
- Clasp of your choice

Techniques
Herringbone Increase, page 19
Peyote Decrease, page 21
Rick-Rack Bangle, page 108

I used
- Dark blue – DB165
- Copper – DB40
- Peach – DB622
- Matte blue – DB756

Sizing
This bangle works up to be a similar size as the original Rick-Rack on page 108, just slightly smaller. However, you do need to allow for your clasp

Getting Started
Using the sizing information on page 108 work out how many sections you will need to pick up. Of the number of sections you need, two will be added slightly differently at the start and end.
So you need to pick up:
- 22A beads for your first section
- 1B and 22A for the next sections
- 1B and 21A beads for your last section

THE STEPS...
Beading the bracelet
STEP 1
Using A beads, bead 5 single peyote stitches, BUT use 2 for the first stitch (matching colours for different rows if needed so the first bead is the same as the last row and the second the same as the new row). Then add a Herringbone Increase between the next 2 beads. Bead 5 single peyote stitches and then a Peyote Decrease (if your counting has worked, this will be over a feature bead). Continue this row until you reach the end, making sure to bead only 5 single peyote stitches.

STEP 2
From now on whenever you start a new row you will bead a 'turn' stitch. Pick up 1 bead of the colour you used in the last row and turn and thread into the last new bead added in the previous row. Then begin your next row. Perform this turn at the start of each row to begin.

STEP 3
Continue beading until your beadwork is as tall as you wish, adding feature beads at the points in the last row to finish.

STEP 4
Attach to your clasp (all those 'turn beads' are perfect to use to do this) and enjoy! □

Step 1

Step 2

Crystal Flowers
Learn how to turn those corners into petals

Materials
- 1 x 14mm round crystal rivoli
- 1g size 11 cylinder beads – your A beads
- 2g size 15 seed beads – your B beads

Techniques
Herringbone Increase, page 19
Peyote Decrease, page 21
Rick-Rack Bangle, page 108

Colour advice
You can really go wild with this project. From using the same colour for both your beads, and also your rivoli, to using a complete mix – the choice is yours

Variations
How many rounds you make on each petal, and how many layers of petals you make, is entirely up to you – this project is completely versatile

TOP TIP
I recommend beading a basic Rick-Rack before you begin so that you are familiar with the ideas

Bezelling the rivoli
Bead a bezel for your rivoli by picking up 36A beads and threading through the first two to join into a circle. Bead 1 more round using A beads then 2 rounds with B beads, pulling tight. Return to your tail thread and add 2 rounds of B beads, making sure to enclose your rivoli before you finish the last round.

TOP TIP
You must Step-Up at the end of every round, even when just beginning your petals, to be in the right place to continue and for the instructions to work

Previous page, top right: For my double-layer big petal flower I beaded 6 rounds of blue A beads then a Point Round of bronze B. For my second layer I did the same but added in extra B beads in the decreasing spaces so that the petals lay flat. Bottom right: In this simple flower Jean used a green crystal with just 3 rounds of A beads and then 1 round of B

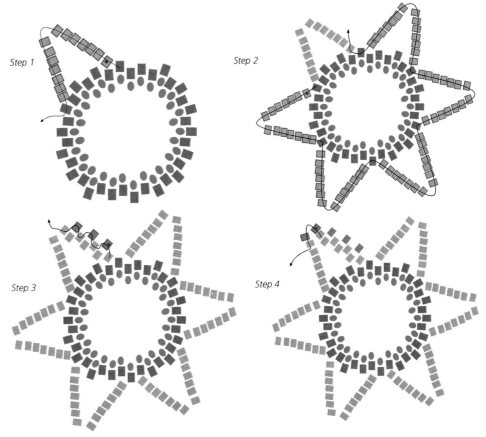

Step 1

Step 2

Step 3

Step 4

THE STEPS...
Beginning the petals
STEP 1
Starting with a bezelled rivoli: Ideally using a new piece of thread (so that if you have a problem you can remove it without undoing your work bezelling the rivoli) weave so as to be exiting the centre round of A beads, coming out of any of them. Pick up 14A beads. Count along the same round you're in and go into the third bead along.

STEP 2
Pick up another 14A beads and go into the bead 3 along (in the same round) from where you are. Repeat this step another 4 times to add a total of 6 petals. When you finish you MUST thread through the first bead added in Step 1.

STEP 3
You'll now bead the third round of the petals: peyote stitch 1A bead into each of the next 3 spaces.

STEP 4
Bead a Herringbone Increase by squeezing 2A beads into the gap between the next 2 beads.

STEP 5
Peyote stitch 1A bead into the next 3 spaces and perform a Peyote Decrease in the next space. If you have counted right you'll now be on the next petal.

In a nutshell!
- Bezel a rivoli
- Use the principles of a Rick-Rack to make petals

Sheila Baldwin, Sarah Parr, Jennifer Buck, CarolNewton and Joanne Doran all beaded incredible Crystal Flowers in their own style

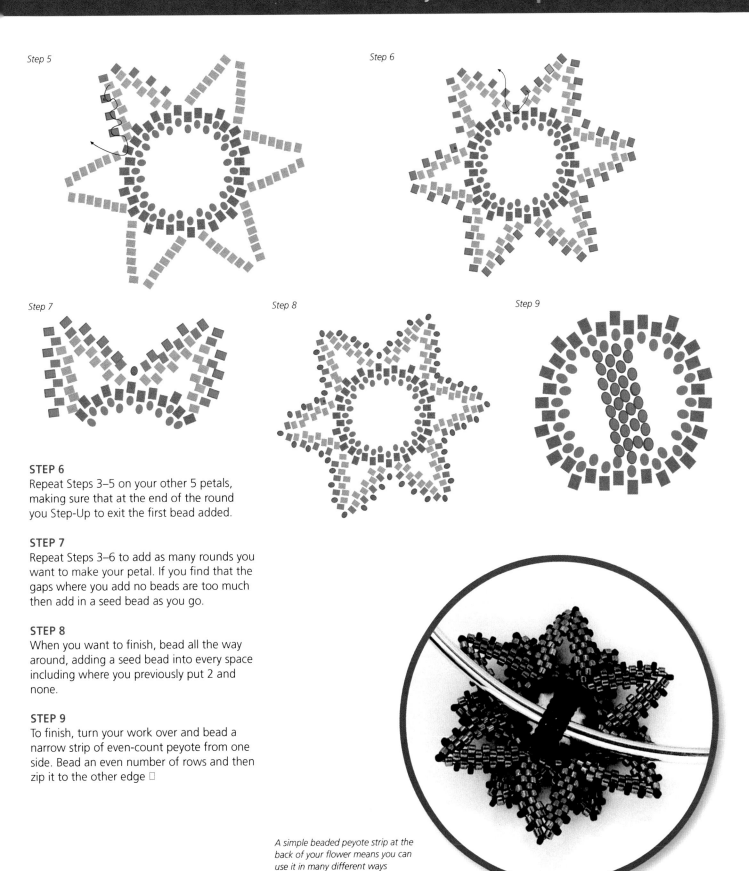

Step 5

Step 6

Step 7

Step 8

Step 9

STEP 6
Repeat Steps 3–5 on your other 5 petals, making sure that at the end of the round you Step-Up to exit the first bead added.

STEP 7
Repeat Steps 3–6 to add as many rounds you want to make your petal. If you find that the gaps where you add no beads are too much then add in a seed bead as you go.

STEP 8
When you want to finish, bead all the way around, adding a seed bead into every space including where you previously put 2 and none.

STEP 9
To finish, turn your work over and bead a narrow strip of even-count peyote from one side. Bead an even number of rows and then zip it to the other edge ☐

A simple beaded peyote strip at the back of your flower means you can use it in many different ways

Geometric Tulip
From the geometric to the floral...

This project is the perfect example of why it pays to play with your work. As I beaded a Rick-Rack bangle I kept rotating it in my hands and wondered what it would look like smaller and if the points were joined. A bit of beading later and I had my first tulip

Materials
- 8g of size 11 cylinder beads for your flowers – your A beads
- 20 x size 8 seed beads in colours of your choice – your B beads
- 32g size 11 cylinder beads for the rope – your C beads

Techniques
- Herringbone Increase, page 19
- Peyote Decrease, page 21
- Rick-Rack Bangle, page 108
- Herringbone Stitch

> **TOP TIP**
> *I recommend beading a basic Rick-Rack before you begin so that you are familiar with the ideas*

I used
- I used a mix of Delicas for my project; changing colours when I felt inclined, so do experiment with yours. The main colours I used were:
- Bronze – DB22
- Red – DB791
- Metallic lilac – DB1012
- Green - DB263
- Turquoise - DB658

THE STEPS...
Beading your flowers
STEP 1
Pick up 22A beads and 1B bead. Repeat this 5 times in total, finishing by threading through the first A bead to join into a circle. Following the basic instructions for beading a Rick-Rack, add between 15 and 20 more rounds for your flower, finishing with adding 1B bead in the place of 2A beads for the last round.

STEP 2
Repeat Step 1 to bead another Rick-Rack. This can be in different colours and have a different number of rounds.

Step 3
Adding 2C beads between each of your B beads

Step 3
Make sure you Step-Up to exit the first C bead added

Beading the rope
Note that the rope only uses C beads. On one of your flowers weave through to exit one of the B beads on the last round.

STEP 3
Pick up 2C beads and thread through the next B bead. Repeat all around the circle to add 10 new beads. At the end of the round, Step-Up to exit the first C bead added.

STEP 4
Using herringbone stitch and only threading into the C beads, add two rounds, each using 10C beads. Make sure to Step-Up at the end of the round.

STEP 5
Bead a round of twisted herringbone by threading down 1 bead on a stack and up 2 on the next. To Step-Up at the end of the round, thread up through 3 beads.

> ### In a nutshell!
> - Bead a small (5 section) Rick-Rack
> - Bead a twisted rope off the Rick-Rack
> - Repeat and then zip ends of rope together

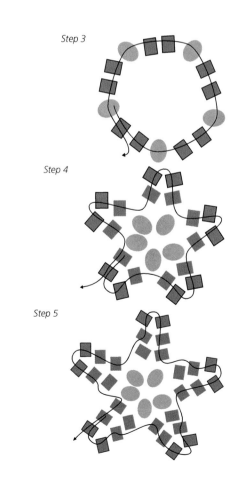
Step 3
Step 4
Step 5

For this simple variation I stitched the ends of some rattail together and added some fringe. Lastly I stitched on my tulip for a long lariat

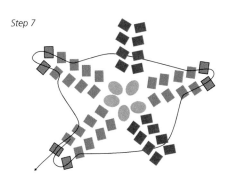

Step 7

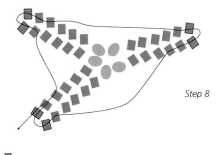

Step 8

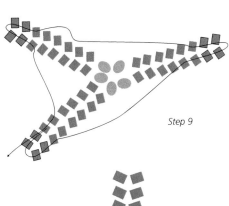

Step 9

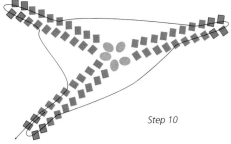

Step 10

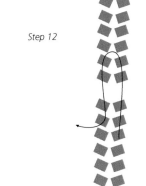

Step 12

STEP 6
Repeat Step 5 for one more round.

STEP 7
Bead a round of twisted herringbone, just as the last round, BUT completely ignore the second stack, instead threading across to the third stack and pushing the second stack inside the rope you're beading. Also do this for what would be the fourth stack. By the end of the round your work will have reduced to contain only 3 stacks. The ones you will push inside your work are red in the diagram.

STEP 8
Bead 1 more round of twisted herringbone, making sure to use only the 3 stacks you will now have.

STEP 9
You'll now move onto 2-drop twisted herringbone where you will pick up 4 beads each time, thread down 1 and thread up 2. At the end of the round you will need to Step-Up through 4 beads to ensure you exit the top of your work.

STEP 10
Continue with 2-drop twisted herringbone by picking up 4 beads, threading down 2, thread up 4. At the end of the round you will need to thread up 6.

Repeat Step 10 until your rope is as long as you need (I made each side of my rope 18 inches)

STEP 11
Repeat Steps 3–10 on your other flower. Finish the threads on one end of the rope.

STEP 12
Bring the two ends of your rope together and zip together by threading up through 2 beads on a stack on the other rope and down through 2 beads- this replicates picking up 4 new beads. Thread down into the top 2 beads of the stack you were exiting and up 4 beads of the next stack.

STEP 13
Continue replicating your twisted herringbone but instead of picking up new beads use those on the end of the other rope.

STEP 14
Repeat this for 3 'rounds' or until your rope is fully joined. Weave away all your thread ends

Two-drop will mean picking up 4 beads at a time

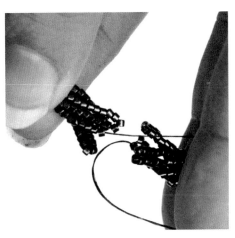

Zipping the two ends of the rope together

When decreasing your rope make sure you bead in front of the stacks you need to ignore

Star Flowers

Turn a Rick-Rack on its head for these floral delights

Materials
- 1g of size 11 cylinder beads
- 5 drop beads

Techniques
- Herringbone Increase, page 19
- Peyote Decrease, page 21
- Rick-Rack bangle, page 108

> **TOP TIP**
> *I recommend you bead a Rick-Rack first to understand how they work*

THE STEPS...

STEP 1
Bead a small Rick-Rack 5 sections wide and 5 rounds high. Bend your work so that the feature beads sit on the outside edge and the Herringbone Increases inside the circle.

STEP 2
Weave to exit a gap where you previously added a Herringbone Increase. Peyote 1 bead into that space and 1 bead into the next 4 spaces.

STEP 3
Weave to be at the next space and zip your work to the 4 beads just added until you are back at your next Herringbone Increase spot.

STEP 4
Repeat Steps 2-3 all the way around to finish your flower.

Moving on
This project is presented to you as a basic idea which you can use, play with, alter and elaborate on. I look forward to seeing what you do with it… □

Step 2

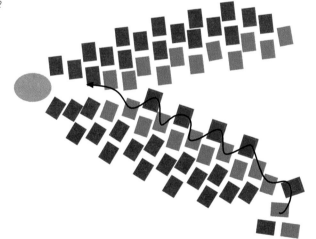

Step 3

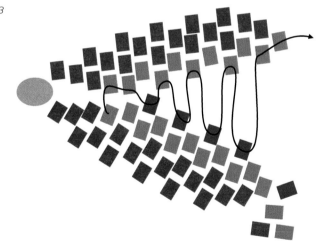

> ## In a nutshell!
> - Bead a small Rick-Rack
> - When zipping, join sides together to make flowers

My final word...
...experiment!

Everything in this book came about through experimentation. Never be afraid to try something out. Even if it doesn't turn into something for weeks, months or even years (or maybe not ever), experimenting is never a waste of time

This book is dedicated to all those who helped me but especially he who knows who he is...

Made in the USA
Middletown, DE
30 July 2020